LLEWELLYN'S
Little Book of
SPIRIT ANIMALS

© Isabel Barney

Melissa Alvarez is a bestselling, award-winning author who has written ten books and nearly five hundred articles on self-help, spirituality, and wellness. As a professional intuitive coach, energy worker, spiritual advisor, medium, and animal communicator with more than twenty-five years of experience, Melissa has helped thousands of people bring clarity, joy, and balance into their lives. Melissa is the author of *Animal Frequency*, *365 to Raise Your Frequency,* and *Your Psychic Self*. Visit her online at www.MelissaA.com.

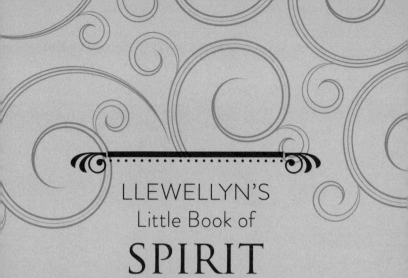

LLEWELLYN'S
Little Book of

SPIRIT
ANIMALS

MELISSA ALVAREZ

LLEWELLYN PUBLICATIONS
WOODBURY, MINNESOTA

FIRST EDITION
Second Printing, 2019

Based on book design by Rebecca Zins
Cover cartouche by Freepik
Cover design by Lisa Novak

Llewellyn Publications is a registered trademark of Llewellyn Worldwide Ltd.

Library of Congress Cataloging-in-Publication Data
Names: Alvarez, Melissa, author.
Title: Llewellyn's little book of spirit animals / Melissa Alvarez.
Description: First Edition. | Woodbury : Llewellyn Worldwide, Ltd., 2018. |
    Includes bibliographical references.
Identifiers: LCCN 2017046390 (print) | LCCN 2017035232 (ebook) | ISBN
    9780738754987 (ebook) | ISBN 9780738752709 (alk. paper)
Subjects: LCSH: Guides (Spiritualism) | Animals--Miscellanea. | Animal ghosts.
Classification: LCC BF1275.G85 (print) | LCC BF1275.G85 A48 2018 (ebook) |
    DDC 133.9—dc23
LC record available at https://lccn.loc.gov/2017046390

Llewellyn Worldwide Ltd. does not participate in, endorse, or have any authority or responsibility concerning private business transactions between our authors and the public.

All mail addressed to the author is forwarded, but the publisher cannot, unless specifically instructed by the author, give out an address or phone number.

Any Internet references contained in this work are current at publication time, but the publisher cannot guarantee that a specific location will continue to be maintained. Please refer to the publisher's website for links to authors' websites and other sources.

NOTE: The information in this book is not meant to diagnose, treat, prescribe, or substitute consultation with a licensed healthcare professional.

Llewellyn Publications
A Division of Llewellyn Worldwide Ltd.
2143 Wooddale Drive
Woodbury, MN 55125-2989
www.llewellyn.com

Printed in China

Dedication

To the animals ... with love

Contents

ॐ

List of Visualizations   viii

List of Tips   viii

Introduction   1

1: The World of Spirit Animals   7

2: Working with Your Spirit Animals   13

3: Wild Animals   23

4: Domesticated Animals   187

5: Mythical Animals   233

Conclusion   279

Bibliography   280

Visualizations

Visualization for Any Animal 12

Visualization with Dragonfly 71

Visualization with Lion 108

Visualization with a Specific Animal 186

Visualization with Cat 192

Visualization with Horse 212

Visualization in a Natural Setting 231

Visualization with Dragon 247

Visualization with Unicorn 275

Visualization at a Moment's Notice 277

Tips

1: How Spirit Animals Can Appear 10

2: Honoring Your Spirit Animals 17

3: Bibliomancy 20

4: Color Meanings 37

5: Elemental Meanings 203

6: Dream Animals 260

After the release of *Animal Frequency*, I was asked to create another smaller book about spirit animals that readers could carry around with them. You're holding that little book in your hands. Because this is physically a smaller book, I couldn't include everything that's in *Animal Frequency*. Some of the changes you'll find are that I've condensed the animal descriptions to one page, left out the full mythology of the mythical animals, and omitted the visualizations for each animal. However, I've *added* fifty more animals in the wild animal section as well as some additional tips and tools to help you connect to your energy animals. It is my hope that both books become part of your library and that you use them often.

My childhood memories of growing up on a farm with many animals is where my understanding and connection to what I call *animal frequency* and *energy animals* began. I work with energy from a metaphysical and spiritual perspective. Through energy work, I help people understand their personal vibration, their own unique frequency, and how they can raise it to higher levels. I teach them to understand their intuitive nature and how to recognize their core spiritual essence so they can progress along their spiritual path and learn their chosen lessons in this lifetime.

I wrote this little book to honor the animals that have honored me with their presence in my life and to help you learn to connect to animal frequency and experience your own spiritual growth during the process. I hope the animals I've chosen for this little book are helpful to you along your path. Animals have always been an important part of my life, and I'm honored to share their messages with you.

The Animal Kingdom

We share Earth with animals, so it only makes sense that we will have interactions with them during our lives. Maybe you've heard that humans tend to be calmer and live longer when they have pets. You can deepen the experiences you have when you connect with animals on a physical, emotional, or spiritual level by also connecting with their frequency, which can enable soul growth within your core essence. You can do this with wild animals as well. While you might not be able to give a wild animal a hug like you would a dog or a cat, you will benefit from their unique frequencies and the messages they bring into your life.

Animals are pure, peaceful, and innocent. They don't harbor resentment, drama, or any of the negative emotions humans sometimes experience. They act and react to the situations around them in order to survive. In the wild, they are predators or prey only because they must eat to live. There is balance in their world. By connecting to their frequency you can find balance in your world. We can relate to being as wild and free as they are, since we often inhibit these primal instincts in our daily life.

The Spiritual World

It is important to understand right from the beginning that animals are spiritual beings, just as we are. Their spirits were created just as ours were. They are part of the universal consciousness, of the Divine, and of the spiritual light of creation. They're not *just an animal* or a *dumb animal*. Do they have a soul? I believe that they do. They have feelings just as we do, and they communicate with one another and with us. They are part of the universal whole, just as we are, they just happen to be in a nonhuman physical body that unfortunately doesn't allow them to form words. They still talk through sounds, through the expression in their eyes, and through the way they physically interact with other animals and humans.

Just as we have spirit guides, angels, and masters to direct us along this path, we also have spirit animals that act as our guides. We have some that are with us for a lifetime, guiding and directing us since our birth, and others that come to us when they're needed for a specific message when we need them the most and then disappear once the message has been received. Many times, spirit animals will bring messages from deceased loved ones from the spiritual realm.

You'll interact with spirit animals on the earthly plane in their physical incarnation and you will also interact with them as guides in their true energy form on the spiritual realm. Regardless of how they appear to you, it is their frequency and messages that are most important and that will assist you. This can lead to a more peaceful and balanced feeling within you, which can enable you to heal, become stronger, and feel empowered on your life path.

Chapter One

THE WORLD OF SPIRIT ANIMALS

I'm often asked if animal frequency is the same thing as animal communication. It is comparable, but there are also vast differences. It is similar because you begin the session by communicating with the animal using intuition, telepathy, thoughts, feelings, and accompanying sounds, which is how they communicate with one another. They're incapable of voicing words, so you have to become part of their world. It's different because you're also working with energy at very high vibrational levels, using all of your intuitive senses as both you and the animal become connected to the Divine. It's being in a place of knowing without words, pictures, or sound; instead, you're surrounded by energy, light, and feelings. It's a different sensation than just doing animal communication—it's more powerful, intimate—and while you'll receive information from the animals, it happens almost instantaneously and with vivid intensity.

When using animal frequency, I go back and forth between the intense level of animal frequency and the normal levels of animal communication that I work with all of the time. As you practice animal frequency, you'll be able to move from one to the other in an instant.

Animal Frequency

Animal frequency is an animal's distinct energy vibrating within their spiritual being, which is contained within their physical body. The frequency of animals tends to be more stable because they don't deal with the drama or stress that we do. Just like we all have intuitive abilities, we all have the ability to identify, attune, and connect with animals using animal frequency. When combined with our own unique frequencies, we can communicate with and understand the reason for the animal's presence.

When working with animal frequency, the first thing you have to do is let go of any preconceived notions that animals are inferior beings because they can't speak like we do, or they don't have feelings, aren't smart, *or it's only an animal*. Remember, you're an animal too. Once you can see an animal as a spiritual being like yourself, then you'll easily connect with them. Animal frequency is important to every one of us because, as spiritual beings, animals bring messages that will positively affect your life.

Animal Totems or Spirit Animals?

Depending on who you speak to regarding the significance of animal appearances, you'll discover animals are called many different things. Some of these terms include (but are not limited to): totems, guardians, familiars, power animals, protectors, and spirit animals.

To me they are all spirit guides, so my preference is to use the term *energy animals* because we're connecting our energy with theirs. I have found that even though spirit animals choose you, and can be unpredictable in their appearances, you can still call upon them in times of need because of the special energy connection you share. You can call on totems too. This also includes mythical beings, so don't be surprised if you encounter a unicorn on your journey.

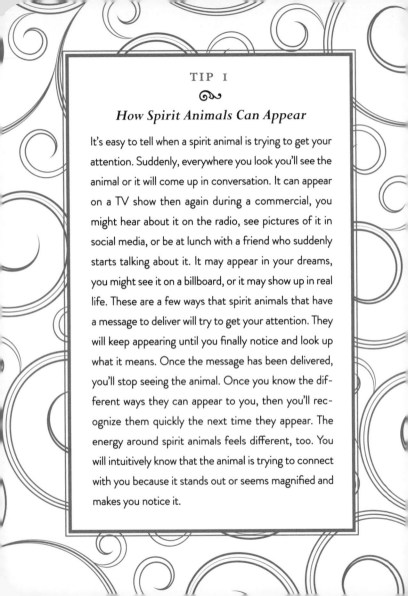

TIP 1

How Spirit Animals Can Appear

It's easy to tell when a spirit animal is trying to get your attention. Suddenly, everywhere you look you'll see the animal or it will come up in conversation. It can appear on a TV show then again during a commercial, you might hear about it on the radio, see pictures of it in social media, or be at lunch with a friend who suddenly starts talking about it. It may appear in your dreams, you might see it on a billboard, or it may show up in real life. These are a few ways that spirit animals that have a message to deliver will try to get your attention. They will keep appearing until you finally notice and look up what it means. Once the message has been delivered, you'll stop seeing the animal. Once you know the different ways they can appear to you, then you'll recognize them quickly the next time they appear. The energy around spirit animals feels different, too. You will intuitively know that the animal is trying to connect with you because it stands out or seems magnified and makes you notice it.

Not What You Expected?

Sometimes the animal that appears to you is not what you might have expected. While you may love tigers or feel a strong connection to the wolf but you're constantly seeing salamanders, ants, or iguanas, then your energy animal messenger is the animal you keep seeing, not the one you like best. Don't ignore spirit animals because you're certain they couldn't possibly be your energy animals. Spirit can appear in all shapes and forms with important messages. Pay close attention to the smallest details.

Animals in Dreams

Have you ever had an animal appear to you in a dream? If so, then you probably experienced your energy animal trying to get a message to you. When Spirit, regardless of the form, is trying to get a message to you and you're not listening, they often attempt to visit your dreams, where you're more apt to give them your attention and listen to their messages. Since animals are strong communicators, if an energy animal is appearing to you regularly, then it's important that you research and really pay attention to determine the message it's trying to deliver because it most certainly has something important to say to you.

VISUALIZATION FOR ANY ANIMAL

Here is a visualization that you can use to connect to any animal. I call it MOVE. First, you are going to use your mind to connect telepathically, then observe the animal, vibrate with the animal's energy, and enjoy being with the animal. So read the visualization and then try it yourself. Close your eyes. Imagine the environment where your animal lives. Are you in a jungle, a cave, or the desert? Notice the quality of the air—is it dry or wet? What sounds do you hear as you walk around? The animal that you've been seeking walks into a clearing in front of you. Now it's time to MOVE. Connect telepathically. What images do you see; what emotions do you feel? Ask the animal to deliver its message. Take a moment to observe how the animal reacts to you. Is it curious? Intimidating? Raise your vibration, your spiritual frequency, fill it with love, and send it to the animal. Feel the connection made between the two of you. Take a few moments to enjoy being in the Divine with the animal. Scratch it, show it that you love it by hugging it, or, if it's small, just hold it in your hand. When the visualization is over, write down the results of your MOVE into the animal's world.

☙

Chapter Two

WORKING WITH
YOUR SPIRIT ANIMALS

Have you ever wondered if your pet was psychic? Or maybe you're not quite sure how to feel an animal's energy. In this section, I'll address both of those topics and teach you how to conduct an animal frequency session. All of these will help you build stronger connections with the animals that come into your life.

Is Your Pet Your Energy Animal?

There are several schools of thought regarding animal totems and pets. Some believe an animal totem can only be a wild animal. Others believe domesticated animals, including pets, aren't actually capable of being totems because they have lost their true wild essence, which in turn lessens the connection to Spirit when they became domesticated. I have experienced powerful energy from pets, past-life memories, and spiritual connections that were just as powerful as my experiences with wild animals. This is another reason I use the phrase *energy animals*. All animals are made of energy, whether domesticated or wild, and we connect with them through energy pathways.

I believe our pets can come back to us after they pass in order to continue to guide us within the physical realm, or, if they choose not to reincarnate, they guide us from the spiritual realm. I've had it happen both ways. You will know when your pet is with you as a guide or an energy animal because you will feel a deeper connection to him/her and will sense it has a greater purpose in your life other than just being your pet. You'll be able to easily communicate telepathically and empathically with this animal. It helps you heal, inspires and uplifts you, and makes you want to be a better person. Its absolute acceptance and love for you will keep you grounded and let you know there is no greater spiritual truth than pure and unconditional love.

Feel the Animal's Energy

It's important to know that you are surrounded by energy and you are energy, and this also applies to animals. Everything in nature has a high vibration. Animals' vibrations are high because they live in the moment. Animals are happy to just be themselves with no worries bogging them down. They eat when they are hungry and rest when they're tired. There are no schedules to keep. They are accepting of whatever life throws their way and don't worry over things they can't change because they aren't judgmental. In order to understand animal frequency, you also have to understand how animals think and how they can communicate with you.

Telepathy is a natural part of intuition used by all species to send and receive images, emotions, and thoughts over distances. You approach the process through feelings of compassion and love to reach out to the animal. When you connect with animal frequency then you are in tune with their needs and are showing them love and respect for their sacred gift. It is truly a gift from the animal to be able to share their frequency.

Start by setting a positive intention and then focusing on the energy animal that you've selected. Open your mind to seeing pictures the animal may send to you or words you may hear or suddenly *know*. In order to really connect your frequency with that of the animal, you have to be very *in the moment* and in tune with the energy animal. When you're connected with your energy animal, you will feel many different things during the transfer of frequencies. You might feel a sense of peace or a calmness come over you, or you may hear a sizzle or static in the connection. Make sure you're aware of how the transfer of energy feels and also how it sounds.

The other part of an energy animal encounter is to be aware of what you were doing or thinking when the animal appeared to you. When you're aligning frequencies, both the message of the animal and the reason for its appearance are important for helping you understand the message. Once you've learned how to connect your individual frequency with an animal's frequency, you'll notice that all animals are more aware of you. They can feel your love, your higher vibration, and that you are aware of them on a soul level.

౨๑

Honoring Your Spirit Animals

It's important to remember to honor your energy animals as often as you can. It is a blessing to be able to connect with your energy animal's frequency, so it only makes sense that you should want to express your gratitude to them for their shared energy connection. There are many ways you can do this. Here are some ideas to jump-start your creativity:

- Share your frequency by sending energy
- Collect statues and figurines
- Share your life with animals
- Support charitable organizations
- Create drawings or paintings of the animal
- Make a vision board
- Write stories or poems about the animal
- Wear jewelry or clothing of the animal
- Watch movies and TV about the animal
- Get a permanent or temporary tattoo of the animal
- Research the animal
- Give gifts to or leave gifts out for the animal

Conducting an Animal Frequency Session

To get started with an animal frequency session, you're going to begin with regular animal communication, which is the sharing of thoughts, emotions, and images between you and the animal. You're going to use your own intuition and telepathy to share with the animal. You'll know what you're receiving from the animal is accurate because your own clairvoyance will be absolutely sure that it is the truth. You don't have to be in the same room with the animal, you don't need a picture of it, you just need to sense its energy to connect with it.

Next, you're going to amp the animal communication into the stratosphere of universal consciousness using animal frequency. As you're exchanging information with the animal, feel your energy—your personal vibration, your frequency—building over your heart until it's swirling with positive intention. Slowly send your energy to the animal. Imagine it as colorful ribbons of pulsating energy leaving your heart and flowing toward the animal. Don't let it touch the animal, but instead invite the animal to share its frequency with you. Soon you'll feel the animal's energy start to build, and then you'll feel it reaching out to you, until your energy and the energy of the animal touches. Now there is an explosion of information moving freely between the two of you. It's an unexplainable, intuitive knowing flowing on intense positive waves of energy as your frequencies merge together. You see what the animal has been through, feel what it feels, and it does the same with you through flashes of images, feelings, hopes, and dreams. All of this is done willingly with feelings of love and trust. It's an intimate, personal, and soulful experience. When the session is almost over, thank the animal for sharing itself with you and pull your frequency back inside you.

How to Use This Book

This book is intended to be a guide to help you learn to recognize and connect with the frequency of energy animals so you can more closely identify with them, which will make it easier to receive the depth of their messages. You should also learn from your own experiences during your frequency exercises by speaking directly to the energy animals, trusting in your own intuition, being present in the moment, and accepting of the messages you receive. Only by doing this will you truly grow on your own spiritual path.

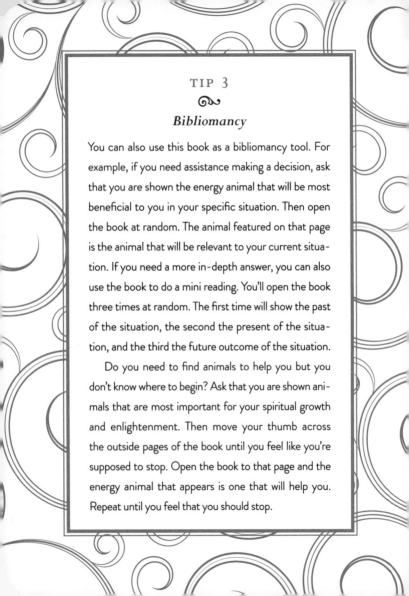

TIP 3

Bibliomancy

You can also use this book as a bibliomancy tool. For example, if you need assistance making a decision, ask that you are shown the energy animal that will be most beneficial to you in your specific situation. Then open the book at random. The animal featured on that page is the animal that will be relevant to your current situation. If you need a more in-depth answer, you can also use the book to do a mini reading. You'll open the book three times at random. The first time will show the past of the situation, the second the present of the situation, and the third the future outcome of the situation.

Do you need to find animals to help you but you don't know where to begin? Ask that you are shown animals that are most important for your spiritual growth and enlightenment. Then move your thumb across the outside pages of the book until you feel like you're supposed to stop. Open the book to that page and the energy animal that appears is one that will help you. Repeat until you feel that you should stop.

The layout of this book is set up as a reference tool. You don't have to read it from beginning to end (but you're welcome to if you'd like); instead, you can quickly flip through the book to find the animal and read about it. This will help you connect to its frequency and understand the message it's trying to deliver when it appears to you or when you decide to seek it out. You can use this book to look up animals you've always felt drawn to, that you're afraid of, or that you are curious about to see what messages they offer. You'll also find pages with tips and visualization exercises placed sporadically throughout this book that will help you identify, attune, and connect to the energy of animals.

If you're ready to get to know your energy animals, to learn from them and receive their messages from the spiritual realm, then dive right in! The energy animals are waiting to meet you and guide you on your journey. Just remember to be open to what they have to say and don't doubt what you're sensing, hearing, or seeing as you connect your energy to theirs. It might not be what you expect but sometimes the unexpected is often exactly what you need. Have fun!

Chapter Three

WILD ANIMALS

Aardvark

Element(s): Earth | Primary Color(s): Brown, gray

Aardvark symbolizes cautiousness and slow progression, digging for what's underneath, adaptability, and change. When Aardvark appears, it is a sign to stop, look around, and make sure the people in your environment are really who and what they appear to be and aren't projecting one image but have different intentions. If you're embarking on a new adventure in your career or relationship, use caution and be certain of the steps you'll take instead of jumping in headfirst and asking questions later.

Aardvark means you need to take some time for yourself in quiet solitude to aid in relaxation and for clarity of mind and spirit, which will enable you to see the truth of situations, reconnect to your core spiritual being, and gain amazing insights and realizations. You accomplish more after dark than during the day. You have thick skin, don't let the negativity of others get you down, and are organized, methodical, and like to stay in control. Your hearing is excellent, and you probably have the gift of clairaudience. Aardvark warns to listen to not only what is being said but what is being insinuated.

Alligator (Crocodile)

Element(s): Earth, water | Primary Color(s): Green

Alligator watches without being seen. It encourages you to do the same. It represents a highly intuitive, creative nature—one you may have been blocking or avoiding. Alligator means you're fearless, have deep emotions, and appear indestructible. Sometimes this means waiting until the time is right before taking action. If you move too soon you could miss your goals. It means to reassess how you're interacting with others. Are you insensitive, cold, and uncaring? If so, alligator is a reality check to change your behavior.

Alligator helps you attract the right people into your life, helps you make deliberate decisions, and assesses the situation before striking. It warns against making decisions before gathering all available information. Alligator can help you keep secrets, maintain your own high standard of ethics, and keep you grounded and emotionally stable. Alligator can also help when you need to keep your mouth shut or if you need to make use of strong jaws and sharp teeth. It can open your flow of creativity to help you come up with new projects, ideas, or inventions.

Ant

Element(s): Earth | Primary Color(s): Black, red

Ant communicates through pheromones, touch, and sound, which means to listen to your own senses as you go about your work. Ant means you're very adaptive and motivated, which ensures success. You take action and make decisions based on what you feel will be best for the group instead of what is best for you. Ant is a sign to work harder to accomplish your goals or an indication that you need a break to rest and reorganize.

Ant means you're an achiever with a team mentality who sees projects through to their completion. You're industrious, creative, and patient. You are one part of the whole and must trust in both your ability to get the job done and in the abilities of those you work with. You prefer structure and order to chaos. Ant teaches others in the colony through tandem running, so an ant's appearance means to look for someone in need of help. Ant means that if you've been isolating yourself now is the time to get back in touch with others. If a queen ant appears to you, it means that you are either in the role of a leader or a parent or you are about to step into that role.

Antelope (Pronghorn)

Element(s): Earth | Primary Color(s): Black, brown, red, white

Like antelope, you think on your feet, tackling problems with ease and finding a resolution swiftly and efficiently. You are very intuitive and can detect the truth of a situation and take the appropriate action. Once antelope makes a decision, it sees it through to the end. If you start something, you see it to completion. Antelope also means new opportunities are presenting themselves to you at this time. Be very aware of what is going on around you and go after any opportunity you feel is right for you.

When antelope appears, it is a sign that you are going to have unexpected changes happening in the very near future. The changes will pop up quickly, so grab the opportunities when they present themselves so you don't lose them. Overall these will be positive and exciting, but you might run into someone who is negative or jealous. Antelope lives in a herd. If you've been avoiding people or are being a loner, try to find others with similar interests. If you're feeling irritable, take some time to be alone and sort things out in your mind. When you're feeling normal again, head back to the herd.

Armadillo

Element(s): Earth | Primary Color(s): Brown

Armadillo means to take the path less followed, to protect your inner self, and to dig deep to get to the truth of your soul. Armadillo is a sign to protect your inner self from the negativity of others. Make sure those around you understand your life rules and stay outside of your personal space. If they cross over your boundaries, retreat within yourself to keep them at bay until you can unearth their true intentions.

Armadillo reminds you to keep your mouth shut about things you don't want spread around the gossip mill. Armadillo warns if you tell too much, it could negatively impact you. Be specific and clear about what you expect from others and stay quiet about your own personal or work situations at this time. Keep your secrets secret. Armadillo means to connect with water to rejuvenate your intuition, sense of trust, and empathic abilities. It can wash away frustration and replace it with a deep calm while giving you the benefits of cleansing on a spiritual level. Armadillo warns not to wear your heart on your sleeve but to keep a close hold on your feelings.

Baboon

Element(s): Earth | Primary Color(s): Gray

Baboon means to express yourself, especially if you feel like you're being taken advantage of or if you're hiding your true feelings about a situation because you fear what others might think. Baboon urges you to let your feelings be known. Baboon is very loud and aggressive, especially when it's upset, and can help you be vocal when you're having difficulty getting your point across and understood.

Baboon lives in tight-knit family groups, keeps itself groomed, and is very protective of its offspring. This means that family and friends that you love are important to you and you'll always do whatever is needed to protect, guide, and show them how much they mean to you. Your appearance is also important, especially when you're trying to move ahead on your life path, so take the time for proper grooming and dressing correctly for any occasion. Like baboon, you tend to talk with your hands and can be very animated, especially when you're excited about something. Also like baboon, you are comfortable in any situation. Your energy is dynamic, your strength of character admirable, and you'll surely be a success in anything you attempt in life.

Badger

Element(s): Earth | Primary Color(s): Black, gray, white

Badger symbolizes a fearless, persistent, and fierce nature. Badger is independent, self-reliant, and, prefers to be left alone. It doesn't hesitate in its actions if confronted. *Badger* means "to never give up." Decide what you want and go for it without delay, pursuing it until the goal is accomplished. Be persistent and fierce in your drive to obtain what you want. This isn't a time to be soft, complacent, or let others fight your battles for you. Be firm, direct, and strong while standing on your own two feet.

Badger encourages you to fight for what you desire through courageous determination. You have excellent communication skills, so use your words; they hold great power. This not only applies to goals you've set for yourself but in defending those you believe in who may have been wronged and the ideals and principles you hold as your own truth. Be firm in your communication with others so there is no doubt of what you want. Better yet, ask for it! Badger warns against eating too much unhealthy food, especially sweets, and now is a good time to monitor your diet and exercise.

Bat

Element(s): Air | Primary Color(s): Black, brown

Bat appears when transformation is necessary. This can be a physical or inner transformation or a move to a new location or career. If you prefer solitude to crowds, you might find yourself participating in group events. Bat encourages group interaction instead of a solitary life. Release any fear, doubts, or hesitations that are holding you back from being a participant instead of an observer and step forward onto a different path. Watch, listen, and think before you react. Maintain your keen sense of observation because it will be an integral part in your development and progress on new ventures.

Bat means you should embrace the positive qualities within yourself and look at the world from a different point of view. It assists when you are transitioning from one phase of your life to another or are experiencing major life changes or small changes in your day-to-day routines. If you're working on your own spirituality, bat can draw the information you need to you, help you understand it, and assist in your spiritual change. If you've been avoiding facing the truth about a situation in your life, bat can help you see it clearly.

Bear

Element(s): Earth, water | Primary Color(s): Black, brown

Bear symbolizes a fierce strength and a gentle nature that is often underestimated. Bear also enables you to see visions and have strong intuition. It encourages you to be your own advisor. Bear often appears when you need to take time away for yourself so you can revive and find your center or balance. It can indicate a need for more rest, extra sleep, and downtime when you're frazzled by life. It can mean you'll need to protect someone or reflect on a situation you're not sure about. There is a need to stick to your beliefs without compromise.

Seeing bear means to look beyond a person's physical appearance to what's inside. Bear also appears when you have lost your way or when you need to reconnect with your inner self at a soul level. To really know your path, you must know your true self. You may need healing at this time, either physically, spiritually, or emotionally, so it's important to find balance and get plenty of rest. You're a survivor with plenty of new ideas and the assertiveness to bring those ideas to fruition. Don't hide, but step out and take what is yours.

Beaver (Muskrat)

Element(s): Earth, water | Primary Color(s): Black, brown

Beaver means to be resourceful and work with intention. Utilize your time and energy in a way that you're not wasting either. Avoid procrastination. Beaver means you're self-sufficient, even though you prefer working with a group. You're loyal to family and friends and a bit wary of outsiders who want to be part of your inner circle. You tend to protect those you love and hold them close, out of harm's way. You're very creative, motivated, and unafraid of hard work.

Beaver's appearance is a sign to move forward with your plans or start the project you've been thinking about. It also means you may forget to take time to relax. Beaver assists when you want to create your dreams in reality. If you've been thinking about starting a business, ask beaver to help you. If you have to finish a job quickly, want to get out of situations where you feel trapped, resolve conflicts with others, clean up, declutter, or reorganize, beaver can guide you through all of these situations so you are successful. Beaver helps when you're overwhelmed and need quiet time to meditate and contemplate your path.

Bee

Element(s): Air | Primary Color(s): Black, brown, gold, yellow

Bee symbolizes accomplishing impossible tasks if you only set your mind to it. Bee means you're too busy and need to rest or you need to stop resting and get busy if you've been procrastinating. You enjoy the sweetness of success. You're often able to keep a busy environment organized and running smoothly. Bee warns against being too quick to temper or stinging too much. Bee is also a sign of hidden wisdom and to look for the wisdom within you.

The queen bee represents birth and ruling over your domain. If you feel you're in a situation where you're not appreciated or are taken for granted, now is the time to create a new environment where you are important, appreciated, and can be the creative being that you are. Bee assists when you have a project or a situation where the outcome seems impossible to achieve. Bee also helps when you're having a difficult time enjoying the fruits of your labor. If you go from project to project without feeling a sense of accomplishment at the end of each one, then you're taking on too much and need to give yourself time to enjoy the success you've earned.

Beetle

Element(s): Earth | Primary Color(s): Black, blue, brown,
green, red, orange, and multicolored patterns

Beetle symbolizes persistence and faith during changes in your life, especially ones that do not mesh with your beliefs. Beetle means changes are coming that will require you to transform in some way. Beetle protects and energizes you, giving you the strength you need to see the situation through to the end. It is time to expand your knowledge and to experience growth within your spiritual self.

Beetle means to keep things simple to make the most progress. You're practical, grounded, and methodical, but you can be introverted and prefer a solitary, contemplative life over one that is hectic and filled with an abundance of people. Beetle is seen as wise and sacred with a deep knowledge of spiritual ideals. It means to notice the small things in life to glean greater knowledge. Beetle helps with spiritual growth, developing life principles, transformation, and manifestation. It is Divine wisdom and finding knowledge from the small things in your life. Beetle encourages you to keep your integrity and to be responsible for your actions.

Black Panther

Element(s): Earth | Primary Color(s): Black

Black panther symbolizes a protective, courageous, and powerful guardian. It means darkness, death, and rebirth, and it connects to the astral realm. When black panther appears, it is a sign that now is the time to reclaim any of your strength and power that you may have given to someone else or lost. You are at home in the darkness, are powerful, and can be aggressive when needed. You are an empathic intuitive who holds your natural abilities close.

Black panther is a sign to embrace your fearlessness and to go after your prey, which may be a new job, a new home, or any other goal. Black panther gives you strength of success. It symbolizes the need to listen more. You can uncover a lot of valuable information by paying close attention to what others are saying without getting so involved in the conversation that you give away your secrets. It assists when you need to heal wounds of the past and gives you the strength to learn from the past and move into the future. It can help you awaken to your clairvoyance, clairaudience, and empathic abilities. It awakens your passion and desire to succeed.

ॐ

Color Meanings

Considering colors you see or feel when you connect with animal frequency can give you insight into the energy animal and can help clarify the message it gives you.

BLACK	ASSERTIVE, BEING IN CONTROL, BIRTH
BLUE	A SEARCH FOR TRUTH, AFFECTION, ANALYTICAL
BROWN	BEING GROUNDED AND DRAWN TO NATURE, HONESTY, NEW GROWTH
GREEN	ABILITY TO SOOTHE, ABUNDANCE, BALANCE
INDIGO	ALL THINGS ARE POSSIBLE, HIGH ASPIRATIONS, INSPIRATION
ORANGE	AGITATION, COMPETITIVENESS, CONFIDENCE
PINK	GENTLE NATURE, GOOD LISTENER, AFFECTION
PURPLE	CONCERN, GREAT DEPTH OF FEELING, HIGH IDEALS AND STANDARDS
RED	CONTROL, COURAGEOUS, CREATIVITY
SILVER	BALANCE, CALM AND CONFIDENT, COMMUNICATION
TURQUOISE	ABUNDANT ENERGY, BEING IN TUNE WITH YOUR FEELINGS, CONSIDERING NEW IDEAS
WHITE	A LEADER OTHERS LOOK UP TO, CHANGE, INNOCENCE
YELLOW	ACTIVITY, COMMUNICATION, CONQUERING CONFLICTS

Blue Jay

Element(s): Air | Primary Color(s): Black, blue, white

Blue jay symbolizes a connection to your higher self and universal knowledge of the spiritual realm. When blue jay appears, you're getting ready to enter a time of growth on a mental or spiritual level. This growth will be long-reaching and can ultimately change your life. It assists when you need to be more daring, need someone to leave you alone, or want to connect to the Divine.

Blue jay can help you be more aggressive in going after what you want if you tend to hold back and wait to be noticed. If you're in a situation where you need to follow the lead of another, blue jay can help you mimic that person while still putting your own unique flair on what you're trying to achieve. If you've gotten too big for your britches, blue jay can make you more humble and modest. It can give you the confidence to create and live the life you want and not settle for the life others think you should have. The only person holding you back is yourself, and blue jay gives you the ability to soar above the others, protect your territory along the way, and reach new heights.

Boa Constrictor

Element(s): Earth | Primary Color(s): Black, brown, green, reds, white, multiple patterns

Boa constrictor symbolizes purposeful actions, intuition, and having keen observation. Boa squeezes its prey not just to kill it but to make it easier to digest. You are like boa in that there is purpose behind everything you do and say. You are a careful planner who strives to obtain the end results you desire by following a carefully laid out plan. Like the boa you move slowly and with purpose, and you know when to put on the pressure to achieve your goals.

Boa is connected to spirituality and the Divine due to its intuitive nature. Boa means you give your all to relationships and expect no less in return. If betrayed, you will walk away and nothing the other person can do or say will make you change your mind. Boa warns against being too possessive and insecure. While it holds on tightly, it's also quick to release and devour its meal. You do the same if you feel you've been let down. Boa means you're always in control, have heightened senses but can get stressed out easily, and have a hard time making decisions. Boa means transformations are coming your way so prepare.

Boar

Element(s): Earth | Primary Color(s): Black, brown

When boar appears, it means that you are on the path of personal growth. It holds the mysteries of the natural world, spiritual strength, and knowledge, and it brings quick resolutions. Boar means you can't be afraid to stand up for yourself, other people, or something you believe in. To do otherwise will inhibit your personal growth. Boar will help you learn from taking a stand and grow in knowledge. Boar encourages you not to hesitate or second-guess your intentions. Listen to your instincts and act accordingly. Follow your own rules, think outside of the box, and never let anyone tell you that it can't be done.

Boar brings out your competitive side, and you're not afraid to take risks to win. If you're feeling down about yourself, boar can boost your self-esteem and confidence. It assists when you need to calm down or get your anger under control. If you're facing a situation where you need to overcome fear, work through problems, or confront someone you've been avoiding, boar can help you handle this with ease. If you're feeling unorganized and out of sorts, boar can help you get back on track. Boar can help bring closure.

Buffalo (Bison)

Element(s): Earth | Primary Color(s): Black, brown

When buffalo appears, it means that you need to reexamine your respect for nature. Look for new ways to understand the natural laws of the universe and make use of the resources available to you to expand your spiritual growth. Buffalo means to appreciate what you've been given. You may not always get what you want but you'll always have what you need.

When a white buffalo appears to you, expect an exceptional transformation that will completely change your life for the better. White buffalo is considered the most sacred living animal and can bring forth miracles. It represents peacefulness and a sense of calmness that connects to your spirituality. Buffalo is a reminder to be respectful to yourself and your elders, family, and friends. Buffalo warns against losing your temper. Buffalo is a sign that good things will come to you but sometimes you have to wait for them. If you try to force an issue, it will probably have the opposite effect than what you're trying to achieve. When you're feeling lost, buffalo can help you find your way through increasing your strength, wisdom, and connection to the sacred.

Butterfly

Element(s): Air | Primary Color(s): All the colors of the rainbow

When butterfly appears, it means you need to add more fun into your life. It can indicate that you're becoming more popular, meeting new people, and embracing a lighter, more carefree attitude. Butterfly means it's time to embrace change, including changes to your way of thinking. It can help you become more spiritually minded. If you've been living a solitary life, come on out of your cocoon and show the world your beauty and light.

Butterfly can mean it's time to add color to your life. If you've thought about taking up painting or another type of art, seeing butterfly means it's a good time to start a new artistic hobby. Butterfly represents letting go of the old and emerging from periods of transition as a new you. It assists when you are contemplating a major change in your life. Butterfly can guide you through the decision-making process and help you choose the right course of action. It can help you be more expressive with your emotions instead of keeping them locked inside the cocoon you've created to hold them. Butterfly gives more vitality and excitement.

Capybara

Element(s): Earth | Primary Color(s): Black, brown, red

Capybara symbolizes calmness, wisdom, and hidden power. Capybara is the world's largest rodent and is related to the guinea pig. It feeds on plants along the water's edge, which means that now is a time to seek your own inner calm by connecting with the energy of water. When Capybara appears, it means to make your current circumstances work for you. If things are going great, then find ways to share your joy with others. If you're struggling, figure out a way to find acceptance and joy in your current situation while planning and taking the necessary steps to change the negatives in your life into positives.

Capybara offers you gentleness and strength, the ability to protect yourself during difficult times, and the courage to change your life for the better. Capybara means you're very social and make friends easily. Connected to the spiritual realm, Capybara urges you to delve into exploring the waters of your own spirituality, understanding that you are one with the Divine, and exploring your intuitive abilities. Capybara warns to take care of your skin because you may sunburn easily or have other skin conditions.

Cardinal

Element(s): Earth | Primary Color(s): Red

Cardinal symbolizes hope, love, and renewal. Cardinal is known for the male's bright red feathering. When cardinal appears, it means that success is coming your way. The brighter the bird, the more success you'll find. Cardinal means you are spunky, vibrant, and filled with happiness and joy. Your energy knows no bounds and you're often on the go. Cardinals can be aggressive when it comes to defending their territory. It lends you this ability when you need to protect what is yours. Cardinal also lends you its song. Both the male and female cardinal have beautiful voices and encourage you to sing your own individual song. When you do, you'll release anything holding you back and will increase your vitality.

Cardinal is also connected to the spiritual realm and is often a messenger for loved ones who have passed on. Cardinal means to watch for signs from spirit, to connect to your ability as a medium, and to pass on any messages you may receive for someone else. Cardinal means to add more color and vibrancy to your life through song, dance, or any activity that makes you happy.

Caribou (Reindeer)

*Element(s): Earth | Primary Color(s): Dark brown
to nearly white*

Caribou symbolizes strength, endurance, and adaptability. Caribou can run up to 60 miles per hour, travel long distances, and adjust easily to new conditions. This means that you'll be traveling in the near future and this trip could take you far from home. Both male and female caribou grow antlers, which symbolize protection of family and recognizing both the male and female characteristics within you. It means the sharing of duties, or working within a group, while maintaining your own personal power.

Caribou means making a decision and then following through with your actions. It symbolizes determination and power of forward movement. Caribou helps you face tasks, especially long-term ones, with a focused and determined attitude, which leads to your ultimate success. Caribou warns of working too much and not enjoying life, of getting stuck in a rut and not experiencing the variety of life. If you're limiting yourself or being repetitive, change direction, learn something new, or take on a new hobby to add spice to your life. Caribou is connected to intuition, prophetic dreams, and clairvoyance.

Just as we have spirit guides,
angels, and masters
to direct us along this path,
we also have spirit animals
that act as our guides.

Catbird

Element(s):Air | Primary Color(s): Gray

When catbird appears, it is a sign that you are a great communicator. You are able to mimic the words of others yet make them your own. Catbird advises to listen closely and put what you've learned to use. Catbird warns that your words can be distorted by others, so think before you speak and make sure you use words that make your intentions and meanings easy to understand so there's no chance of misunderstandings. Catbird also warns that what you say may become public knowledge. If you don't want something to be known, don't say it.

Catbird appears when you're going to be meeting new people. Listen closely to what they say and learn from them. It assists when you need to be clear and concise in your communication, whether it's the written word or speaking to someone. Catbird warns against bringing too much attention to yourself because it may be the kind of attention you don't want. Catbird can also help you deal with nosy people. It can give you the words to politely say it's none of your business without offending others. It is also a reminder that you shouldn't be putting your nose in where it doesn't belong.

Caterpillar (Inchworm)

Element(s): Earth | Primary Color(s): Brown, green

Caterpillar symbolizes hidden potential, strong use of the senses, and the promise of a beautiful tomorrow. Inchworm means to be make sure your path is clear in purpose, take accurate measurements, and take smaller steps to get to your goals. When caterpillar appears, it is a reminder that everything in life happens in its own time, not the instant you want it. Live in the moment, moving at your own pace while taking time to smell the roses along the way.

Caterpillar means to keep what you're doing, planning, and creating under wraps until you're ready to reveal it in its magnificent completion. Revelations should not be discussed during the transformation process. Be one with the process and trust that what you are doing is necessary for growth and change. You do not need anyone else's opinions at this time. Trust in yourself. Caterpillar reminds you that in order to transform, you must release the old and embrace the new. Let go of what no longer serves you and embrace the new manifesting in your life. Inchworm's appearance means to slow down, you're moving too fast.

Catfish

Element(s): Water | Primary Color(s): Gray

Catfish symbolizes looking deep to find truth. People may not be what they seem or there is information hiding beneath the surface that you need. When catfish appears, it means that someone is pretending to be someone or something that they're not. This can happen in social media settings or in your daily life. Catfish is a warning to keep your eyes and ears open for the truth and to use your intuition to uncover answers in order to protect yourself. It means to be choosey in the people with whom you're interacting. Don't follow along blindly.

Catfish also means that while you don't waste your time or energy on unnecessary tasks, now is the time to really hunker down. You may be on a deadline where time is of the essence. Catfish means you're an emotional person who can sometimes find slights when none were intended. If there are people who are pulling you down into the depths of their despair on a continuing basis, now might be the time to back away from them for a while. It's one thing to be a caring, supportive friend and another thing to have a negative friend trying to bring you into their darkness. Choose wisely.

Centipede (Millipede)

Element(s): Earth | Primary Color(s): Black, brown

Centipede symbolizes movement. With its abundance of legs, it can move quickly and indicates forward motion in life and the ability to do many things at once. Centipede means taking care in what you say and the manner in which you say it to avoid misinterpretation. Its antennae symbolizes a connection to all things intuitive. The appearance of centipede means that you're likely to meet someone in the near future with whom you'll have a close psychic or past-life connection.

Centipede means you'll come into your own and achieve success later in life rather than earlier. Safety and security is important to you. It assists when you want to have more coordination, for example if you're learning to dance. If you feel disorganized, out of sorts, or at odds within yourself, centipede will help you feel grounded and find balance and harmony within. Centipede warns to get out of the spotlight and retreat to where you're most comfortable. You need this time to reevaluate and recharge, to plan, and to create. Centipede is believed to ward off bad luck and negativity.

Cheetah

Element(s): Earth | Primary Color(s): Black, tan, white

Cheetah symbolizes speed, stealth, and strength. You may need all three in the near future and your life may feel like it is on fast-forward. This is a temporary situation and will slow down to a normal pace soon. If cheetah appears, you need to respond to situations without hesitation. It means something you had on the back burner has become a top priority and you must deal with it now.

Cheetah means to stay grounded as you move with top speed. You must remain focused and pursue your goal with intensity, stealth, and speed while using your instincts, intelligence, and courage to see it through to the end. Cheetah reminds you that once you've attacked a situation, take the time to recharge and recover from the effort to bring you back to center and a place of balance. Cheetah can show up as a message that you need to become more active and get into better physical shape to avoid health issues. Cheetah will lead you down a direct path and won't let you stray. Cheetah warns that sometimes you must overcome a struggle in order to succeed.

Chickadee

Element(s): Air | Primary Color(s): Black, gray, white

Chickadee means that you need to be aware of the people around you. It can warn you when someone isn't being honest and remind you to always tell the truth no matter how uncomfortable it might make you feel. Chickadee influences personal and business relationships and is a clear sign to communicate effectively, to be diplomatic, and to refrain from getting into a conflict.

Chickadee means that now is the time to be open and excited about ideas, projects, proposals, and the people in your personal life. Now is not the time for secrets but time to open up to creativity and your true feelings. Chickadee's song is unique and, once heard, is easily remembered. It means you too can be as vocally expressive as chickadee and as hard to forget. It assists when you're feeling down about yourself, if your self-esteem is low, or if you're being overly critical about what you've been able to accomplish in your life, chickadee can help you overcome all of these things and see the brightness within them. You are more than you think and chickadee can help you be more accepting of yourself, flaws and all.

Chimpanzee

Element(s): Earth, air | Primary Color(s): Black

Chimpanzee shows up when you need to use your language skills, intellect, and understanding of social hierarchy to solve problems or to close a negotiation. Chimpanzee relies on community and a network of associates to make life easier. You are able to do the same, especially in business, in order to land new deals, expand your market, and grow your company. Now is the time to show aggression only if absolutely necessary.

Chimpanzee warns against being short tempered at this time. Keep silent, show compassion, and find the balance within the situation in order to achieve the results you desire. Chimpanzee means that you have a wide variety of interests and it might take you a while to settle on a career. Chimpanzee means that you have a plethora of knowledge, are very intelligent, and are a keen observer but warns that now is not the time to try to force these qualities on others or to show them off. You'll be more successful if you practice understanding and patience. You are also curious, which means you would be a great inventor. Your gentle nature draws others, just be careful that they're not taking advantage of you.

Chipmunk (Ground Squirrel)

Element(s): Earth | *Primary Color(s): Black, brown, red*

When chipmunk shows up, it's time to get busy storing up for winter. Don't waste time. You've much to do, so you'd better get busy doing it! If you've been thinking about investing or increasing your material possessions, now is a good time to start. If you're considering new ways to make more money, start implementing them so you will see results soon. Chipmunk means to stay balanced between work and your social life. If you overdo either one you'll be out of balance and may be ill-adjusted.

Chipmunk advises to pay particular attention to how people are speaking. Listen for the inflections in their voice, how it rises and falls, and whether they're speaking in soft or loud tones. It assists when you're being overly talkative. Sometimes it's better to let others take the lead in a discussion instead of you doing all of the talking. Chipmunk also means to wait before telling secrets that aren't ready to be revealed. If you're unsure what someone is talking about, or if they're saying one thing but mean (or feel) another, chipmunk can help clarify their intentions.

Clam

Element(s): Water | Primary Color(s): Gray, yellow

Clam lets you know that silence is golden at this time. Don't let others know what you're up to and be careful. If you've got the next great idea, don't share it. Instead protect it. That said, don't go overboard either. Clam means you're an amazing person with incredible talents but you don't let the world see your true self. You're much more comfortable hiding your talents and abilities within your shell so others don't make fun of you or steal your phenomenal ideas.

Clam means that sometimes you have to open up in order to shine. It's difficult for you to trust, but when you do, it's done wholeheartedly. It assists when you're in a situation where you don't know what to do. If you're feeling out of sorts, it can help you get back into the rhythm of your life through mind, body, and spirit. Clam can help you build inner strength and tap into strong emotions. Even though it retreats into its shell when it's threatened, clam can help you become more outgoing. You have a lot of plans and positive intentions about the things you want to accomplish but you sometimes don't follow through.

Cobra

Element(s): Earth | Primary Color(s): Black, brown, red, yellow

Cobra is symbolic of gracefulness, speed, and ancient knowledge. It is the most venomous snake in the world, and is seen as sacred and connected to the Divine. Cobra is also indicative of death, rebirth, and eternity. When cobra shows up, it means that you need to get to know yourself better. Now is the time to make an effort to connect to your higher self, to understand yourself at a soul level, and to move forward on your spiritual path. If you need to make a quick decision, ask cobra to help. It can boost your self-esteem, boost your confidence, and show you the way to embracing your own greatness.

Cobra can help you hide in the shadows when stealth is needed. Cobra is exceptional when it comes to finding out the truth of any situation and can guide you to that truth. Cobra means you should learn more about your past lives because something from one of them could be affecting you in your current lifetime. Discovering and acknowledging that past life can help you release fears and problems you may be currently experiencing. Cobra helps you begin again to become all that you want to be.

Once you can see an animal

as a spiritual being like yourself,

then you'll easily connect with them

Cockroach

Element(s): Earth | Primary Color(s): Brown

Cockroach symbolizes cleaning away the old to make way for the new. When cockroach appears, it means that you may soon encounter a change in your living conditions. You may experience an unexpected need to relocate, whether it's your own decision or a forced move. You'll face this change with ease because of your excellent survival skills and adaptability. You never give up on the things you want. You can weather any storm, bear any burden, and come out of trying times ahead of the game. You're very sensitive to the needs of others due to your empathic nature.

Your preference is a quiet life without a lot of change or activity but when those things do come, you handle them with ease. If you notice you're depending on others too much or are feeling pressure from your peers, cockroach can help you learn to rely on yourself more and make your own decisions instead of falling in with the ways of a group. Cockroach's appearance means you need to take some alone time to let go of stress, rejuvenate, and do some spring cleaning both in your home and within your person.

Conch

Element(s): Water | Primary Color(s): Pink

Conch means to speak the truth with power, conviction, and belief. You are a leader, and others look up to you for your wisdom and spiritual enlightenment. Sometimes people may not want to listen because it's easier to avoid the truth than face it, but your words are delivered in such a way that they will understand and benefit from them. Conch means you're not afraid to toot your own horn if it means helping another person. While you prefer living in your shell, you'll come out to inspire and teach others. Your strength is in your balance, wisdom, and ability to see within the spiritual realm and to share the knowledge you've gained. You're an inspiration to others and help them develop their own abilities and walk their own spiritual path.

Conch means you have musical talent as a singer or in playing an instrument. The spirals within the conch's shell are an indication that you are able to pull deep within yourself, connect with your inner consciousness, and experience enlightenment. Conch symbolizes the awakening of the heart to love. It can assist you in affairs of the heart, with relationships, and with family.

Coral

Element(s): Water | Primary Color(s): Every color imaginable!

Coral appears when you need to share with others. It may be material goods, advice, or just a shoulder for someone else to cry on. You are a strong person mentally and emotionally, can weather the turbulence of another's emotions, and are a great listener. When you give advice, it is filled with the wisdom of the ages, even if you don't realize it. You innately know what to say to put someone at ease and to calm their storm. Coral urges you to embrace the artist within you. Creativity in all forms acts as a stress reliever.

When coral appears, it is warning you to nourish yourself so you don't become weak. Being productive is also a sign of coral. New projects and opportunities are coming your way. Coral symbolizes spiritual growth, emotional support, and practical understanding of spirituality and the human psyche. You intuitively know what steps to take in any given situation, so don't doubt yourself. Coral means to make a deeper connection with your own feelings. It encourages you to see beauty in every aspect of your life, to trust in universal guidance and accept the happiness and rewards that come to you.

Cougar (Mountain Lion, Puma)

Element(s): Earth | Primary Color(s): Brown

When cougar appears, it means to be very decisive right now. It's not a time to be wishy-washy. Make a decision and stick by it. Stay strong, don't procrastinate, and be clear in what must happen in the situation. Handle it with courage and determination. Have faith that you will achieve the desired results. Cougar lets you know that some people may not like your take-charge attitude and will criticize what you're doing. The best way to resolve this situation is to get that person more involved, give them more responsibility, and take their opinion to heart. They may feel like prey when they should feel like an accomplice.

Cougar means to own up to and learn from your mistakes. Don't let others hold you back from taking on challenging situations. You know how to be in charge of your own life, so do what you need to do but don't hurt others along the way. Cougar assists when you need to make decisions and you feel torn and unsure of what to do. It gives you strength and patience during hard times and helps you see how to handle yourself with grace. If you're doing too much, cougar can teach you balance.

Coyote

Element(s): Earth | Primary Color(s): Gray, red

When coyote appears, it means you need to laugh more. If you're stressed out and taking everything too seriously, try to lighten up a bit. It also indicates trickery, a joker, and being able to laugh at your own mistakes. Like the coyote, people may feel that you're hard to understand because you tend to see humor in difficult situations. It means you're clever and can often find easy ways to skirt around difficult situations.

Coyote can enhance your verbal skills so you speak effectively, are engaging, and add humor to what you say. If you're bored, stuck in a rut, or can't find motivation, take coyote's advice and do something fun that makes you happy. If you're struggling, coyote can help you see a clear path to get out of difficulties. Coyote means to never think in absolute certainties. Coyote warns not to make a simple task overcomplicated. Be flexible, adaptable, and make small adjustments when life doesn't go as expected. Coyote encourages you to look at the positive instead of the negative, live fully in the moment, never take anything for granted, and appreciate the joy in your life.

Crab (Crayfish, Lobster)

Element(s): Water | Primary Color(s): Red

When crab appears, it means you're about to experience rejuvenation, regeneration, and transformation. Just as the crab grows within its shell and then molts if off, prepare to enter a cycle of spiritual, mental, or physical cleansing that will result in a complete renewal in some area of your life. This is a time of emotional growth as well. You may connect deeply with your intuition and healing abilities and experience more emotional depth and understanding of yourself.

Crab assists when you need to feel more protected. Just as it has a hard, protective outer shell, it can lend this feeling to you. If you need to hold on to something, ask crab to help you with its strong claws. If you're feeling held back, then ask it to show you what is holding you back so you can let it go and free yourself. Sometimes you can purposefully hold yourself back from reaching your goals without realizing you're doing it. If you find yourself in a situation that's not good for you, lobster and crayfish give you their ability to move backward, out of the situation, at a quick rate of speed.

Crane

Element(s): Earth, air | Primary Color(s): Brown, gray, white

Crane symbolizes discretion, grace, and balance. When crane appears, you may be put in a position where you know secrets that you must keep. Silence is a top priority. Crane means you're a private individual who prefers to wander away from the crowd instead of following the next new craze or showing off how much you know. You aren't a worrier and take life as it comes. Crane is associated with agelessness, with longevity, and with wisdom. This means you're wise beyond your years and people may consider you an old soul. You hold your age well and are often thought to be younger than you are.

Crane gives you its elegance in movement, and you're often an excellent dancer. Focused determination and picking your battles make you an excellent businessperson who is prosperous and sees potential where others may not. Crane warns against being so focused on what you're doing that you ignore everything else. Crane is a sign of good fortune, of new opportunities and success, and of abundance and plenty. You'll achieve all that you desire if crane is by your side. It is the balance and connection between mind, body, and spirit.

Cricket

Element(s): Earth | Primary Color(s): Black, gray, green

When cricket appears, it means that you are incredibly lucky. Everything seems to always go your way and you're always in the right place at the right time. Cricket also means you are aligning to higher vibrational energy on a regular basis and are using your inner song to enhance your energy. Cricket means that you're coming into your own, aligning with your inner self, and making great progress in understanding your spiritual path. Embrace your intuition because you're more accurate than you realize. Make sure you're grounded and balanced when doing intuitive work. Believe in yourself and the impressions you're receiving.

Cricket means singing even in the darkest of times. Cricket's song can bring you out of darkness and into the light. Cricket also means that now is the time to let go of any emotional baggage weighing you down. Release the past to embrace the future. Crickets are thought to mean you're going to have some type of financial windfall. It's considered bad luck to kill or put outside a cricket that chirps inside a house.

Daddy Longlegs (Opilionids)

Element(s): Earth | Primary Color(s): Gray

Daddy longlegs is a name to describe Opiliones, which are closely related to mites but look like fragile spiders with long legs. They aren't spiders because they don't produce silk or webs and are nonvenomous. The name daddy longlegs has also been used to describe the crane fly and cellar spider. Opilionids are connected to ancient knowledge. There is a Scottish fossil of one that is 400 million years old.

When daddy longlegs appears, it means that you'll be congregating with a large group in the near future. This could be family, friends, or work related. Daddy longlegs means to make sure you're in balance in all aspects of your life. If any area is taking up too much of your time, or you're putting in a lot of effort and you're not making any forward movement, then now is the time to make changes to bring back harmony and balance. Opilionids mean to tap into your creativity. This is a good time to come up with a new idea to pursue, a new business to start, or a new project to begin. If you're looking for a new hobby, consider painting, writing, or music.

Deer

Element(s): Earth | Primary Color(s): Brown, white

Deer symbolizes a gentle nature, sensitivity, unclear direction, and sacrifice. Deer connects to the purpose of your soul. This is a time of awakening, of realizing your true self and the path you must take in this lifetime. Deer inspires you to be aware, focused, and observant. Deer means you prefer a simple life filled with quiet and peace. You get overly stressed in hectic environments. You'd rather stay in the background and out of the spotlight but your beauty, gracefulness, and compassionate nature pulls you to the forefront time and time again.

Deer alerts you to danger, aggressive people, or negative situations, and it advises you to distance yourself from them. When deer crosses your path, it is a sign that you need to reevaluate your feelings. Now is the time to make changes. Let deer show you a calm, peaceful path where you can turn any negatives into positives. Deer means there are opportunities coming your way and this time, instead of saying no like you usually do, say yes. Step out of your comfort zone to enjoy a phenomenal experience. Take time to truly live.

Dolphin (Porpoise)

Element(s): Water | Primary Color(s): Gray, white

Dolphin symbolizes curiosity, mindfulness, meditation, and enlightenment. Dolphin shows you both the fun and depth of any situation. It encourages you to look for meaning in all you do because, by considering all aspects, you will become enlightened. Dolphin symbolizes freedom, balance, and harmony in all things. Dolphin shows up when you need to lighten up and find the fun in your life. It appears when it's time for you to begin a quest to understand your own spiritual being and to find enlightenment. Don't leave any stone unturned and crash through every wave until you can settle within yourself to be more mindful and calm.

Dolphin means to pay special attention to your intuition. If you get an impression, don't blow it off as your wild imagination, instead, take it for what it is and own it. Dolphin means to get creative. Start a project, fill it with your feelings and emotions, unleashing the creativity within you, and then display it for all to see. Dolphin helps you recover from emotional wounds by tapping into your healing abilities. Connect to your joy and your inner truth and be empowered.

Dove

*Element(s): Air, earth | Primary Color(s): Gray, white,
and a wide variety of other colors*

Dove symbolizes peace, love, and devotion. The white dove symbolizes purity, surrender, and hope. Dove is a reminder to be peaceful and calm. If you've been out of sorts, fighting with someone else or just on edge, dove can help you find balance and calm down. It is a sign to embrace those you love. Make sure they know how you feel about them. If you've been taking someone for granted, show your love and appreciation to them in a grand way. Let them know how you feel. Dove also means to make amends with anyone you've been arguing with or haven't spoken to in a long time due to a misunderstanding. Be the bigger person, the peacemaker, and let go of the past hurts so you can lift the weight of the situation from your shoulders.

Dove encourages you to eat healthy foods and to cleanse, both physically and spiritually. Dove means to be hopeful for the best positive solution to any problem you encounter. You are the epitome of love and positivity. All will be made right within your world if you embrace dove's messages. Dove is a sign of new beginnings and can help you with yours.

Dragonfly (Damselfly)

Element(s): Air, water | Primary Color(s): Blue, green, red, yellow

When dragonfly or damselfly appears, it is a sign to tap into your intellect and emotions. You can seem unpredictable at times, but this is what gives you an edge in competition. You're a game changer—a passionate person wrapped in a beautiful, iridescent package. People often don't see past your beauty to the depth within and that's when you're able to surpass their expectations. Dragonfly means to show off your abilities and strive for success.

Dragonfly means you need to add lightness to your life. Don't get bogged down in the heaviness of the world but be the light, airy being that shines in a multitude of colors. To be light means to be free and to be free means to be connected to the wisdom of the universe. See the goodness and light within others and encourage them to do the same. Dragonfly means to find balance, harmony, and meaning. Dragonfly also helps when you're going through a personal or spiritual transformation. Becoming enlightened is a key element of dragonfly. It encourages you to find that which will help you grow into a higher place along your spiritual path.

Visualization with Dragonfly (Damselfly)

Imagine ... You're working outside, tending to your yard, when a green dragonfly lands on your arm. You consider the beauty of its wings, its slim body, and big eyes. It stays put for a minute then takes off again. A while later, another one lands on the end of your rake. You're filled with delight but don't dare move so you can observe it. You feel excited that they've chosen to connect with you and now find yourself looking for them. Later, while driving to the store, you're at a stoplight and feel as if you're being watched. You look out of the driver's side window and see a baby red dragonfly sitting on the glass peering in at you. You smile broadly and say, *Hi, little guy!* Just as the light changes color it flies away. You feel a lightness within your soul and a deep connection with dragonfly energy.

❧

Eagle

Element(s): Air, water | Primary Color(s): Brown, white, yellow

When eagle appears, it means that you are not limited in any way, so do not let anything hold you back. You are a free spirit who needs to take time to connect with your own spiritual nature. There is vision, focus, and power within you. Now is the time to let it fly free into the world. You see the bigger picture and the long-term goals and strive with determination to control your path and meet each opportunity with action and skill.

When eagle shows up, it means you are protected or you are going to be protective of someone. This could be physical or emotional protection or simply a compassionate shoulder. You command authority wherever you go and can present an imposing presence for those who don't know you. For those who do, they know you are an inspiration and a guardian and have a deep sense of community pride. You are a natural leader that other's respect and follow. Eagle is a reminder that your keen insight will be needed in the near future. Eagle energizes, gives you an expanded view of situations so you can see what direction you should take, and encourages you to soar to great heights.

Earthworm

Element(s): Earth | Primary Color(s): Brown, red

When earthworm appears, it means that you have to take time to look at the little things in your life. Scrutinize and absorb the minute details—turn them over and work them out as if you were tending a garden. Only in working through a situation can you bring it to a successful resolution. Cultivating and tending your life with love, joy, and happiness allows for new growth. You may feel that the efforts you're making are small and inconsequential but your actions will reshape your environment.

Earthworm means you need to dig deep and move slowly and methodically in order to make substantial, lasting progress. You are persistent in your attention to detail. A natural caretaker, you find joy in helping other people and animals, and you often fight for causes that will positively impact the environment. Earthworm encourages you to clean house both physically and emotionally, letting go of anything clogging up your system. Earthworm warns against people who may try to take advantage of you, so be wary of anyone who suddenly has a keen interest in you and what you're doing.

Eel

Element(s): Water | Primary Color(s): Brown. Moray eels come in a wide variety of colors and patterns.

When eel appears, it means you are in hiding or need to take a step back into the shadows to regroup. You are about to embark on a journey. This may be traveling in the physical world or a spiritual journey of the soul. Either of these voyages will result in a dramatic transformation within you on an emotional or spiritual level. Some may call you electrifying. People are attracted to you because of your positive energy. You adapt to new situations easily, have an inner defense mechanism that you supercharge when you feel threatened, and are able to slip away unnoticed if you so choose.

If you're looking for a new opportunity—whether a new relationship, career choice, or business venture—you're most likely to encounter it after dark. Eel reminds you to rest instead of burning the candle at both ends. It assists when you need to observe a situation without being part of it. Eel can help you dig out of the mud of circumstances that wears on your energy and make the changes needed to leave it behind. It encourages you to keep quiet, slip away, and think instead of being too vocal.

Elephant

Element(s): Earth, water | Primary Color(s): Gray

Elephant symbolizes inner strength, a wide range of emotions, and the physical ability to overcome obstacles. When elephant appears, it means you need to be more communicative and committed to your personal relationships. Take the time to really listen to what others are saying. What feelings hide beneath their words? Be gentle in nature, intelligent in your choices, and willing to be deeply dedicated to the person. Once you truly listen, you will develop a deep understanding of one another. Don't assume the people you care about know how you feel. Tell them, show them, and value their presence in your life.

Elephant means to push obstacles out of the way; don't let anything hold you back from what you want to achieve. Elephant tends to only look forward, which is a sign not to have a narrow focus but instead look all around you and be aware of your environment. Elephant gives you its determination—nothing can stop you from achieving your desires. You push past obstacles that stop others in their tracks. If you're venturing down a path of spiritual enlightenment, elephant is the perfect animal to guide you.

Emu

Element(s): Earth | Primary Color(s): Black, brown, gray

Emu symbolizes the emergence of inner strength, wisdom of the ages, and the quest for such knowledge. When emu appears, it means that you're about to embark on a spiritual quest that will change the way you think about life, your soul purpose, and universal energy. Emu means that you're a hard worker who takes pride in a job well done. You're respectful of others, humble, and down to earth. People reach out to you because they feel you are trustworthy and will give them excellent advice.

In the wild, the male emu cares for and raises the young. This means there will be a male figure appearing in your life to guide you or, if you are male, that you will be called upon to offer support and guidance to someone. If you've felt like you've been locked down, emu urges you to take time to get out in the world and explore to rid yourself of restless feelings. You like the adventure of moving around and you're naturally curious. If you can find like-minded souls to accompany you on the journey, that's even better. Emu helps you get rid of any preconceived notions so that you can learn and grow without restriction.

Firefly (Lightning Bug)

Element(s): Air, earth | Primary Color(s): Black, orange, yellow

Firefly gives you hope when all seems dark. It lights your way as you travel life's pathways. Firefly means that while you may seem plain in the daytime, when you glow, you radiate your inner light for all to see. If one were to look closely at you, they would see this light in your eyes, but not everyone will take the time. Your inner beauty is a wondrous sight to behold. Your kind and caring nature can light the way for anyone who is lost or in need of guidance. For this reason, you're often the shoulder someone cries on and are the first to give a hug even if the person says they're fine. You see deeply and can tell they're going through something and need a hug.

Firefly profoundly speaks to our spirit, the essence inside our bodies, inviting it to attract the light of other similarly minded people. Firefly's light doesn't contain heat, which is a sign to take life at a regular pace instead of going too fast and burning out too soon. Firefly encourages you to live a simple life. Firefly means to light your inner fire and to be passionate in reaching your goals.

Flamingo

Element(s): Air, earth, water | Primary Color(s): Black, pink, white

When flamingo appears, it is a sign for you to either become part of a team or a group with similar interests or participate in more social events. If you're too social, retreat for some alone time and steer clear of hectic events, especially if you're over-reacting or becoming stressed out when in the company of others. Flamingo is often connected with psychometry. Your intuitive knowing from touching objects is an integral part of your life. If you're out of balance, this ability can be affected and your impressions may not be as clear.

Flamingo's mouth is designed to siphon out the food. This is a sign that you should siphon out the important things in your life and discard any muck that is holding you down. Flamingo often sleeps or stands with one leg tucked up close to its body. Scientists believe it does this to conserve body heat due to the coldness of the water. This is a sign to conserve your energy and rest when you're fatigued instead of pushing yourself too hard. Assists when you need to find balance. Flamingo suggests letting some things go to regain your equilibrium.

Flea

Element(s): Earth | Primary Color(s): Brown

When flea appears, it means that something is bothering you or you feel that someone is taking unfair advantage of you, but you're not exactly sure why you're feeling this way. Flea means to take the time to examine the cause of your irritation and a way to alleviate it, otherwise it will continue to increase in urgency. Flea urges you to be resourceful and determined to get to the bottom of the situation. You may find yourself on edge, irritable, and quick-tempered when flea is around. Instead of being focused on projects at hand, you jump from one to another without getting much accomplished. Once flea's message is delivered and the source of your aggravation is dealt with, you'll go back to your normal way of being.

Flea urges you to take advantage of new opportunities coming your way and motivates you to make changes in your life. Flea lives on blood, which is a warning not to let other people drain you physically, emotionally, or energetically. Be aware of their actions and assertive in stopping them. Flea is sensitive to vibration, which means it can help you raise your own personal vibration, your frequency.

Fly

Element(s): Air | Primary Color(s): Black

Fly symbolizes change, growth, and persistence in reaching goals. When fly appears, it means you are letting small things irritate you. Instead of focusing on those little things, look at the bigger picture from a different perspective to see clearly. Fly means change is coming, and it will happen in an abrupt manner. You may be caught unaware, but your survival skills and ability to make quick decisions and take action will allow you to overcome any negativity to prosper. Fly never gives up. It keeps going after its goals regardless of how much of a pest it's making of itself. You have this same quality, so if you realize that you're annoying others, quickly change your course of action to ensure success without making enemies along the way.

Fly assists when you need to look at a situation from a new perspective. Fly has two eyes but within each eye there are more than four thousand smaller eyes. The incredible eyesight of fly can help you see situations from multiple points of view all at the same time. This can give you great insight into people, projects, and situations where you need to see a broad range of possibilities.

Fox

Element(s): Earth | Primary Color(s): Black, gray, red,
silver, white

When fox shows up, it means to spend more time with your family. Participate in family outings and activities and just spend quiet time with one another. Fox has incredible eyesight, which is a sign to watch what people do more than listening to what they say. Actions speak louder than words and at this time you'll glean useful information through sight instead of sound. Fox means you should stay in the background unnoticed.

Fox warns to be wary of people who don't have your best interest at heart. Are they being sly and cunning? Trying to trick you? Fox means to be alert to these qualities within yourself but to also look for them in others. They can be very revealing of the individual's true intent. You're a great problem-solver, can intuit the intentions in others, and are unafraid to take risks. It assists when you want to stay out of sight and observe the activities of those around you. If you're traveling as a family, fox is a great animal to ask along to help keep you safe. If you find yourself in any kind of predicament that you need to get out of, fox's ability to slip away will aid you.

You can deepen the experiences
you have when you connect
with animals on a physical, emotional,
or spiritual level by also
connecting with their frequency.

Frog (Toad)

Element(s): Earth, water | Primary Color(s): Brown, green

When frog appears, it is a sign that you need to focus on one thing and do it well. Frog has a tendency to jump from one project to another. It warns that now is not the time for being unfocused but instead you need to concentrate on the most important situation in your life and give it all of your attention. It's time to be serious, hold your ground, speak your mind, and let your emotions out. This is a time of cleansing, of transformation, and of future growth. Relationships can be restored at this time. New opportunities can be locked down.

Frog means you have a knack for giving great advice because you really listen to someone's problem before speaking. You tend to have close and meaningful relationships with others. You're the friend who is reliable, dependable, and who will always show up when called. You love with abandon and with your whole heart. There's no middle road with you. If you don't like something, you don't like it. You don't pretend or hide your feelings. Assists when you need to release negative emotions and doubt. Frog can help you create new beginnings for yourself.

Fruit Fly

Element(s): Air | Primary Color(s): Black

When fruit fly appears, it means to make the most of what you have in order to survive. Fruit fly means you are going through a transformation, which may be difficult, and will result in a rebirth. Fruit fly gives you the ability to see situations from a unique perspective, to notice the little things in life, and to take that which annoys you and look at it positively. Fruit fly has different colored eyes, which means you see life from angles that others often miss. Just like fruit fly, you are a survivor. Even if things are falling apart and in a state of decay, you can find that morsel within that, with care and attention will grow and change into something wonderful.

Fruit fly means you're quick to make needed changes. You don't second-guess or take a wait-and-see attitude. You know what needs to happen so you do it. Fruit fly most often appears when you need a change in your life to boost your spirits or to lead you in a new direction. It shows you exactly how strong you are and how to survive when you think you just can't. If you've had a disagreement with someone, fruit fly can help you clear the air with grace and calmness.

Giraffe

Element(s): Earth | Primary Color(s): Brown, white, yellow

Giraffe symbolizes making new connections, keeping your head up, and trusting your intuition. Giraffe appears when you're experiencing trying times. Your broad perspective allows you to see more than most. You look for the positive in every situation, and you are graceful, tactful, and patient that it will work out. You're not bothered by small things. You hold yourself to a higher standard, going the extra mile to help others or to accomplish your goals. You tend to have a pleasant personality and are tenacious when striving to reach new heights. People notice your inner and outer beauty. You tend to stand out in a crowd with your elegant grace of being.

Giraffe means to listen to your intuition. You're a leader with a high level of awareness. Giraffe gives you a long-range plan by increasing your vision. You easily communicate with those around you with gentility and patience. Giraffe keeps you on your toes, always looking and planning for the future. You'll stick your neck out to help a friend or when you feel someone is suffering from injustice. Assists when you strive to reach greater heights of success.

Gopher (Groundhog, Woodchuck)

Element(s): Earth | Primary Color(s): Brown, gray

Groundhog symbolizes digging in, looking deeply, and not accepting things as they seem on a superficial level. When groundhog shows up, it means that it's time to get moving, be more ambitious, and really labor to achieve your goals. Sometimes getting what you want requires hard work. Groundhog moves more than seven hundred pounds of dirt to create its burrow, so to achieve results you'll need to be diligent, stay focused, and not give up. Groundhog urges you to keep things clean. When your living environment is clean, energy flows better and there are fewer blockages around you.

Groundhog is an indication that you need to take responsibility for the things you do (or don't do), the choices you make (especially if they affect someone else), and the things that you say. You are accountable for yourself, so don't play the blame game and put fault on others. Groundhog means you're drawn to spirituality, metaphysical topics, dream analysis, and developing your intuitive abilities. You enjoy studying new material on these topics, which in turn helps your own spiritual growth.

Gorilla

Element(s): Earth | Primary Color(s): Black, silver

Gorilla symbolizes leadership, respect, and honor. Gorilla means to recognize that you command attention wherever you are and because of this, you must show the regal qualities of this noble animal in all that you do. Gorilla warns against being overly aggressive. Instead, be diplomatic and simply wait. You are a good leader and know that good things come to those who wait. You're a team player, often the leader who encourages others to be the best that they can be in every situation.

Gorilla means you take your responsibilities seriously and are confident and decisive in the leadership roles you have taken on. While gorilla means you can be aggressive, especially if you feel that someone you're protective of has been wronged, these episodes are short lived bursts of anger. Once they're past, you don't dwell on them. Gorilla means you're constantly on watch, you know what is happening around you even when others think they've pulled the wool over your eyes. Your intuitive nature, clairaudience, and sense of balance guide you. Gorilla warns against being too dominant or materialistic.

Grasshopper

Element(s): Air, earth | Primary Color(s): Brown, green,

orange, yellow

Grasshopper symbolizes being a unique individual. Grasshopper can jump twenty times the length of its body. This means you can't let your size hold you back from making great strides in your life. Grasshoppers are small, but they eat sixteen times their weight every day. This is a warning to watch your diet so you don't overeat or to make sure you're consuming enough to maintain your health.

Grasshopper appears when you're about to experience a dramatic positive change in your life. It urges you to leap at opportunities because they may have once in a lifetime potential. Your natural rhythm and pacing is on point. You can soar by trusting your decisions instead of second-guessing. You're willing to go off the beaten path and to find uniqueness hidden in unconventionality. This is the part of your character that will open new doors to wondrous possibilities. Right now, you have so many doors and windows opening all around you that you're unsure which way to jump. Take a moment to look around, trust your feelings, and take that leap. You'll be happy you did.

Grouse

Element(s): Earth | Primary Color(s): Black, brown, red, white

When grouse appears, it means you need to take time to dance. Lose yourself in the music, letting your body move freely to its rhythm. This will allow you to connect to your true essence. Allow your mind to be free, without worry or stress, and be at one with the sound around you. Grouse means everything has its place in your life and when things get out of place, you might freak out just a little bit. Stay calm and put everything back where it goes. You're deeply attuned to patterns, rituals, and your own specific way of doing things. Just remember the world isn't going to end if things don't go according to plan one day.

Grouse warns against being too rigid instead of going with the flow. When you're out of sorts, grouse can help you return to center, preen, and get back into the majestic flow of your dance. Grouse helps you to manifest by showing you how to use movement, intention, and performance to attract what you want to come into your life. Try creating your own dance or hand movements to add power to your intention during manifestation exercises. This increases the flow of energy to you.

Hare

Element(s): Earth | Primary Color(s): Brown, gray

Hare symbolizes independence, survival, and speed. It is a sign of abundance, fertility, and good fortune. When hare appears, it means you are different than you appear. You have a stronger core essence than others give you credit for. While you prefer to handle disagreements with finesse, you'll fight hard if necessary to get your point across and to defend others or your territory. This is often a surprise to those around you because they didn't know you had it in you to react in such a take-charge manner. You're sensitive, independent, and tend to prefer solitude to group activities.

Hare urges you to take quick action when opportunities arise. Don't overlook the obvious because you want to see something different from what the situation really is. See the truth in the matter, then make a deliberate, intelligent decision. Speed is important to you right now. There are situations coming your way where you're going to have to think fast and take quick actions to be successful. Don't overthink what you're doing. Hare warns to be wary of who you trust, especially in new endeavors.

Hawk

Element(s): Air | Primary Color(s): Brown

When hawk appears, it means you're taking the lead, you have a vision of something you want to achieve, or you're embarking on a spiritual quest for enlightenment and personal growth. Hawk means you can reach great heights as you accept new opportunities. Hawk connects you to the higher realms, where you can interact with spirit guides, angels, and the masters. Your clear vision lets you see accurately into the Akashic Records. This spiritual quest is a life changer, and, once you've opened to Spirit, you see existence from a different perspective. Hawk's ability to soar in the open sky symbolizes you soaring in your new knowledge.

Hawk encourages you to maintain focus in your life. Don't get distracted by trivial things. Continue to reach for the stars, aim high, and fly swiftly to reach your goals. When you need to be flexible but are having a hard time bending, hawk can help you loosen up. Hawk can help you navigate any twists or turns life throws at you by swooping you out of the way. Hawk also helps you face challenges head-on by plunging into it and grabbing hold with sharpness and strength.

Hippopotamus

*Element(s): Earth, water | Primary Color(s): Black, gray, pink
(hippo's milk is pink)*

Hippopotamus symbolizes intuition, set patterns, knowing what is underneath, and protecting oneself. When hippopotamus shows up, it means you need to act on your intuition. Don't overanalyze it or question if what you're receiving is correct. Hippo means you tend to be grounded and don't get caught up in hype. You like to create patterns of behavior and stick to those patterns.

Hippo's appearance means now is not the time to stray from your path. You may feel drawn to distraction but push that feeling aside and focus on what you're doing, where you're going, and your ultimate goal. Hippo lets you see what's underneath the waters. If you're searching for answers, take a better look at what's hidden. That's where the truth will be found. Hippo means you can easily find balance between your physical being and spiritual being. Abundance surrounds you.

Hippo assists when you need stability in your life. Hippo can help you analyze situations and find the balance in all things. If you're starting a new project, hippo can help you stay focused on your path without distraction.

Hummingbird

Element(s): Air | Primary Color(s): Blue, gray, green, red, but can be any color

Hummingbird symbolizes lightness of being. It means enjoying life to the fullest, drinking in its sweet nectar. It is holding those close to you closer, loving with abandon, and being present in your life. Hummingbird is considered one of the most aggressive bird species, regardless of its tiny size. When hummingbird shows up, it means to stand up for yourself and don't let others intimidate you.

Hummingbird gives you speed, and you often do things quickly. Sometimes you have to slow down like hummingbird, too. To you, this means that while you move quickly, you can't wear yourself down. Make sure you take time to recharge before taking flight again. Hummingbird can fly both forward and backward, and it can hover, which means you go with the flow, adapt quickly to changes, and take the time to stop, look, and listen. Hummingbird encourages you to embrace the playfulness inside you. It's essential to your well-being to find a balance between going a hundred miles an hour and sleeping. Sometimes you just need to slow down without actually stopping.

Hyena

Element(s): Earth | Primary Color(s): Black, brown

Hyena means to be sensitive to your words, laughter, and actions at this time. Hyena's call sounds like abrasive laughter, which is a sign that you need to be careful right now so that you don't give the wrong impression. Hyena means that you prefer the road less traveled. You embrace and honor your own uniqueness and go out of your way to do things differently because it's part of your spiritual essence. If you're pressured into following rules that you don't agree with, then you can become snappy and quite difficult to be around.

Hyena means to understand that there are rules about everything and being asked to abide by them isn't dishonoring your true self, but is part of your growth in the earthly realm. Hyena means you have a great sense of humor, don't take yourself too seriously, and can bring a smile to most anyone. Hyena means you're able to size someone up in an instant. Your intuitive nature is highly honed and you never doubt your impressions when it comes to someone's true intentions. Hyena means you're a natural athlete, so if you've been too much of a couch potato lately, now's the time to get moving.

While you might not be able
to give a wild animal a hug,
you will benefit from their
unique frequencies and the
messages they bring into your life.

Jackal

Element(s): Earth | Primary Color(s): Brown, red, tan

Jackal symbolizes travel, protection, and unexpected opportunities. In ancient Egypt, the jackal was the spirit who guided the newly deceased into the next world. This means that you are about to enter a new chapter in your life. You may be moving to a new location, changing jobs, or getting married. Jackal means that life as you knew it is changing so dramatically that you'll never see it in the same way again. All of these changes are positive and in forward motion. If you feel as if you're hanging on to any negativity, jackal can help you release it, lighten up and see the positives, and move forward.

Jackal means that you're always alert to what is happening around you and can sense danger long before it arrives. This means you would do well in any type of security job or detective work. You're clever, intelligent, and use your witty nature to find out information that others might prefer to keep hidden. Jackal is a scavenger, which means you have its ability to find the hidden jewels or most resalable items at a yard sale. Jackal warns that you can tend to be moody and evasive at times.

Jaguar

Element(s): Earth, water | Primary Color(s): Black, brown, white, yellow

Jaguar symbolizes moving without fear through the unknown. When jaguar appears, it means to move forward with stealth and use your intuition and good communication skills. Set your goal; use your authority and strong willpower to steadily move toward accomplishing what you've set out to do. Your beauty, skill, and independent strength of character will help you make positive forward progression. You're secure, self-confident, and have high self-esteem. You're not afraid to go after what you want.

You tend to take situations and people at face value instead of always looking for a hidden agenda. When you need to look deeper into a situation or are having a hard time trusting someone, use your intuition to guide you. Jaguar encourages you to reclaim your inner power through fine-tuning your intuitive abilities and soul empowerment. Jaguar's beauty is good camouflage for its intense inner fierceness. People may not realize the strength, cunning, and stealth you carry inside. You may use your beauty to help you achieve your goals but you'll fight for what you want or need.

Jellyfish

Element(s): Water | Primary Color(s): Blue, red, yellow, and all other colors

Jellyfish symbolizes to stop trying to force things in your life and instead go with the flow, analyze your emotions, and whether you're moving forward with purpose or drifting on the waves. When jellyfish appears, it is a sign to begin again. Get back to the basics and find your balance. You're very adaptable, but if you make things complicated, you can slow your own progress. Jellyfish means to let things happen in their own time, don't try to force your will on situations.

You're open and honest but sometimes come across as too blunt or appear tactless, even if it's unintentional. Your words can sting and cause undue upset if not spoken with finesse. Be sensitive in your approach to obtain positive results. Jellyfish means to trust your inner self. You are connected to universal wisdom. Jellyfish warns that it is easy for you to get dehydrated. When working or enjoying being outside, make sure you stay hydrated by drinking plenty of water. It assists when you're stressed out, aggravated, impatient, or feeling on edge. Jellyfish means things are looking up in your life.

Jerboa

Element(s): Earth | Primary Color(s): Tan

The jerboa is known as the world's smallest rodent and the pygmy species is only one to two inches in size. It has exceptionally long back legs and can leap up to nine feet and run up to fourteen miles per hour. Jerboa means to look for meaning in the little things in life. Now is a time to see that which often passes you by unnoticed. Jerboa lives in desert regions, so it easily blends into the background of sand. This means to make sure that you're not blending in too much instead of making a statement. There are times when you need to do both. Now is a time when you need to speak out instead of remaining quiet and in the background.

Jerboa means you are able to attain great heights with little effort. Choose the things you want to achieve in life and go for them. You'll be successful in all that you attempt. Jerboa is a reminder to drink enough water. In the wild they may live their entire lives without drinking water, instead they get water within their food. Pay attention to your water intake at this time, especially if you're working outside, so that you don't get dehydrated. Jerboa means that you do your best work at night.

Kangaroo

Element(s): Earth | Primary Color(s): Gray, red

Kangaroo means to leap over problems, stay grounded, and move on. Don't look back or regret the steps you've taken. You have a deep connection to the earth, a stable foundation on which you stand (both personally and spiritually) just as kangaroo's foundation is its large feet. If you've lost belief in yourself, kangaroo reminds you to reassess to recognize your truth. Know who you are at your core, a truly unique and wonderful being of spirit, and believe in yourself.

Kangaroo encourages you to stay close to the ones you love most during times of difficulty. They offer a support system that will enable you to be the best you can be. Kangaroo also means your life may be jumping in a different direction soon so stay focused on what's going on around you. As you reach for your goals, this isn't the time to battle obstacles head-on. Just go around, or over, them. It assists when you need forward momentum. If you've gotten stuck in past situations or are letting negativity get you down, kangaroo encourages you to leap forward into positivity. Kangaroo encourages you to stay on your path.

Katydid

Element(s): Earth, air | Primary Color(s): Green

Katydid symbolizes intuition, raising your frequency, and a greater connection to the Divine. Even though they have wings, katydid doesn't usually fly. They tend to flutter to the ground and then they'll climb back up into the trees. This means that the path you're on is one where you'll need to continue to climb, step by step, until you reach enlightenment. Sometimes if you're feeling that you know all there is to know about metaphysical topics, the universe just might push you off a leaf so you flutter down and make the climb again and learn a lesson in meekness. It's important not to get your head in the clouds when it comes to understanding and sharing your knowledge of the Divine.

Katydid means you easily adapt to your surroundings and change isn't a big deal for you. Instead, you flow with what life brings your way. This is a time of spiritual growth for you. Learn as much as you can and let others guide you. Katydid means not to blindly accept what others say as truth. Listen, research, and make up your own mind about what is truth to you on a spiritual level to make great leaps forward on your path.

Koala

Element(s): Earth, air | Primary Color(s): Gray, white

Koala means that you've been holding the weight of the world on your shoulders for a while and now it's time to relax and let go of stress. Koala can sleep for twenty hours a day, which is a sign you need to catch up on your sleep. This would be a good time to take a vacation, or even just a day off, to catch up on rest and relaxation. Take a day to do nothing. Koala means to pay special attention to what you're eating and drinking. Add more vegetables, especially leafy greens, and more water to your diet.

If you've been thinking about doing a short-term detox program, this is a good time to start. Koala helps you know when you need to move slowly and methodically in order to make discoveries or to complete a task. Koala means you're empathic and attuned to a higher frequency. It's time to move higher into the treetops where the vibrations move even faster in order to understand the true nature of your being. When Koala appears, it means to remove drama and enjoy the quiet for a while. A short rejuvenation will allow you to see situations clearer and make decisions easier to make. Koala warns against being too naive.

Komodo Dragon

Element(s): Earth | Primary Color(s): Brown, green

Komodo dragon symbolizes trusting your instinct, survival, and connection to the earth. Komodo dragon means that you are embarking on a new adventure. This could be a new relationship, job, or a physical move to a new home. If you fear the upcoming changes, komodo dragon will put your worries to rest. It lends you its strength of purpose, its warrior energy, and the stealth needed to survive.

Komodo dragon means that change is a normal part of life and that you need to grab every opportunity available at this time because each will make a positive impact on you. It means letting go of that which no longer serves your greater good, whether it's a job, a person, or a situation you've been involved in. Komodo dragon urges you to become more passionate instead of being emotionally level. When you're happy, show your joy. When you're angry, let it out. If you're sad, cry. Releasing emotions instead of holding them deep inside is healing and freeing. Komodo dragon is connected to earth frequency. This means that you may be traveling to another region in the near future, where you'll have the opportunity to attune with nature.

Ladybug (Asian Lady Beetle)

Element(s): Air | Primary Color(s): Black, orange, pink,
red, yellow

Ladybug symbolizes luck, fortune, happiness, and protection. Ladybug means to live life to the fullest every single day. When ladybug appears, it means you're about to have a fortunate change in your life. Ladybug reminds you that you're protected from the negativity of the world, shielded by your own positive defensive shell.

Ladybug warns not to stay hidden in that shell but to come out to ascend to new heights. It's easy for ladybug to stay inside where it's safe, but to open its wings, allowing itself to be vulnerable, is when the greatest accomplishments are made. Ladybug reminds you that sometimes you have to expose your inner self in order to fly. Ladybug is connected to spirituality and the development of your internal core essence. Your spiritual values are strong, so you need to take time each day for meditation, even if it's five minutes to reconnect to your spirituality. Ladybug assists when you've been deliberating over a choice, helping you see the direction to take. If you want to bring more abundance into your life, ask ladybug for assistance.

Leech

Element(s): Earth, water | Primary Color(s): Black, brown

Leech symbolizes patience, purification, and connection with universal energy. Leech is well known as the vampire of the animal kingdom because it lives off of blood. When leech appears, it can mean that someone is pulling on your energy and lowering your reserves because they don't have your best interest at heart. Sometimes there are things happening behind the scenes that you may not see immediately. Leech means to take a good hard look before making any dramatic decisions.

Leech can also mean that you're in the process of healing. Even today doctors often use leeches in modern medicine to help heal skin graphs and to treat burns. You may be getting over a bad relationship or trying to decide what to do about a problem at work. Leech means to look at a situation with clear understanding. Leech can help you see the reasons behind what happened and show you how to move forward. Leech warns you to avoid selfish behavior or leeching off of someone. Now is the time to stand on your own feet, be responsible for your own actions, and to move forward on your own path.

Lemur

Element(s): Air, earth | Primary Color(s): Gray, white

Lemur symbolizes family, traditions, and getting back to your roots. Lemur is associated with the Divine and urges you to dig into spiritual, paranormal, and metaphysical topics. You understand that even if you don't see something, it doesn't mean it isn't there. Your abilities are strong and lemur will help them grow even more, especially your abilities as a medium. You are gifted with being able to communicate with spirit, guides, and those who have passed on. Utilizing this gift, you help both those on the other side and those left behind.

Lemur means to search for answers to the things we don't understand by keeping an open mind to all sorts of possibilities. Lemur means that now is the time to make plans so that you can reach your desired results with ease. Without plans, you may veer off the path and waste precious time finding your way back. Lemur helps you enjoy the simple things in life, release clutter, and enjoy taking things easy. Lemur enables you to speak your thoughts in a direct manner. Your words pack a punch and often take others by surprise or make them think. If you want a direct answer to a question, ask lemur.

Leopard

Element(s): Earth | Primary Color(s): Black spots,
orange, yellow

Leopard symbolizes boldness, beauty, and strength. Patience and persistence are virtues of leopard that enable it to hunt in the moment. Like leopard, you too live in the moment instead of dwelling on the past or worrying about the future. Leopard urges you to accept your uniqueness, to embrace your strengths, and to reclaim your own power, for the power of leopard runs deep. It is a swift, bold knowing of your soul essence, of being all that you are. Leopard means you know yourself well, and you have a keen insight into others. You see them as they are, the truth of their being, and you simply know them in a Divine way.

Not much gets past you and you tend to make others nervous, which makes them talk a lot and give away their secrets. Yet you stay quiet, without letting them know what they have just disclosed. Leopard enables you to see visions in dreams and when you're awake. Your clairvoyance is very strong and if you've been ignoring it in the past, now you must embrace it and make it your own. It's not going to go away so accept that it is part of you.

Visualization with Lion

Imagine ... The roar of the lion resonates throughout the zoo. You feel it rumble through you and you're not even close to the lion enclosure yet. Heading toward the sound, you feel entranced by the majestic nobility of the lion's roar. You catch your first sight of the elegant beast around a bend. It is patrolling, watching over its pride of lionesses. It roars again, the sound is loud and strong. This time one of the lionesses answers the call. You notice that the reply came from a different direction. Looking over, you see a mother lioness with three cubs following her. She only comes part way into the opening and looks up at the male lion. The energetic connection between the two is strong. It feels like arcs of lightning zinging between them. She gives him a soft roar before returning with her cubs to the safety of the brush. Satisfied, the lion lays down on the rock and goes to sleep.

‿

Lion

Element(s): Earth | Primary Color(s): Brown

Lion appears when you're about to step into a leadership role. It means you need to be more visible and in the spotlight and you need to take a dominate role in the situation. Lead, don't follow. Delegate, don't do all of the work yourself. Lion also means to learn from the lioness. In the pride, the lioness is responsible for raising the family. By looking at how the lioness multitasks, you can learn how to bring harmony to your work environment by teaching those you're responsible for how to work in the most productive manner. If a lioness comes to you, it is to show you how to gain balance between work and your home life.

Lion also means you're not being as productive as possible. You may be lying around or goofing off instead of doing the work you need to do. Lion assists when you need to increase your personal power. It can help you relax and recharge by releasing nervous tension, aggression, and anger. It can give you the courage and assertiveness to face problems head-on instead of moving around them. Lion also warns you when a situation is getting out of hand or is threatening your personal and emotional strength.

Lizard (Gecko)

Element(s): Earth | Primary Color(s): Brown, green,
also multicolored

When lizard appears, it means to look for your hidden gifts. Seek your inner visions through meditation or ask that you are shown information while dreaming. By considering your dreams and aspirations, you can bring the most positive ones to light and you can see what is holding you back. Your gifts of rejuvenation will help you through difficult times.

Lizards are cold blooded and enjoy time in the sun. They grow during their entire lifetimes and will shed their skin when they need to grow more. This means that you too absorb the warmth around you and grow throughout your life. You are continually learning and experiencing both personal and spiritual growth. You listen to your heart, aren't ruled by ego, and can regenerate when needed. Of the more than 5,600 species, the only one with vocal cords is the gecko, which means you communicate well through body language. Lizard means you have to connect to your imagination, for that is where your dreams live. If your forward motion is slow, imagine what you want and go for it to get back on pace.

Loon

Element(s): Earth, water | Primary Color(s): Black, white

Loon symbolizes looking into the depths for the truth. When loon appears, it means you need to look within. Are you being overly sensitive, hiding out from others, or letting your imagination run wild? Loon can help you bring all of these situations back into balance. While loon prefers solitude, it isn't a completely solitary creature. It does enjoy being around others, as do you.

Loon is connected to the spiritual world and moving between the physical and spiritual realms. This means you need to embrace your intuitive abilities. You may have been fighting them for a while; maybe even wishing they'd go away. They're part of you and always will be. So instead of fighting them, embrace them. Life will start to flow easier when you do. It's also time to begin work on your spiritual growth. Explore new concepts to see if there is more out there that makes sense to you. When you're ready to learn, the lessons will appear and loon can show them to you. Assists when you need to communicate in a distinctive manner. Loon can also help you bring your hopes and dreams to fruition.

Lynx (Bobcat)

Element(s): Earth | Primary Color(s): Brown, gray, white

Lynx symbolizes possession of ancient knowledge, mysteries of the universe, infinite wisdom, and truth of being, and is the guardian of secrets. When lynx appears, it means that you must be careful not to disclose secrets others have confided to you and that you intuitively know the secrets others hide. You might know their fears, things they've done, or deceptions they've made to themselves and others.

Lynx means you are the keeper of secrets, thus, you should never tell what you know. You have the inner strength to remain silent in all situations. You are at a high spiritual vibration, in tune with your core essence, and, above all, are honorable and wise. People, including strangers, feel at ease with you and trust you due to your inner light and often tell you things they'd never tell anyone else. At times, people may also feel awkward in your presence because they intuitively know that you see them as they really are at a soul level. They unconsciously sense that you know their secrets and they're right. You tend to speak your mind, but you're also cautious around people. You do your best work at night.

Manatee

Element(s): Water | Primary Color(s): Gray

Manatee means to get in touch with your emotions. Instead of holding your feelings inside, let them out. You could choose to write your feelings down, create a song, or simply think about how you really feel about things. Once you are in tune with your emotional self, and are clear in your feelings, then you can move forward on your path. Bottled up emotions or denying your feelings can hold you back from reaching your own greatness.

Manatee is symbolic of a gentle nature. Its slow forward movement under the water means that you must always look ahead, even if it's taking you longer to reach your destination than you'd like. Manatee means acceptance of yourself, of others, and of situations that are beyond your control. It's time to have faith in yourself that you can achieve all that you want in life. If you've had trust issues in the past, manatee can help you overcome the fear of trusting again. Manatee encourages you to trust in yourself most of all. You have all that you need within you but you must nurture your inner self to become all that you can be.

Meerkat (Mongoose)

Element(s): Earth | Primary Color(s): Brown, white

When meerkat appears, it means that you have to watch out for danger and those who don't have your best interest at heart. Meerkat has built up its immunity to venoms, which allows them to eat scorpions, snakes, and other poisonous animals without fearing illness or death. Meerkat urges you to shore up your defenses against those who may mean you harm.

Meerkat doesn't have fat stores, so it must eat daily in order to survive. This is a reminder that you shouldn't skip meals and to take your bodily nourishment seriously. If you need to slim down, develop muscle, or just get back into a healthier way of living, meerkat can help you achieve this goal. Meerkat also reminds you to be aware of your position in life. If you want to achieve higher ranks or elevate your status, meerkat can teach you how to climb the ladder of success. You are a natural leader with strong social skills and can handle many tasks at once. You work well in a group environment and enjoy management. You crave adventure and have a vivid imagination. Meerkat assists when you need to expand your vision.

Mole Shrew

Element(s): Earth | Primary Color(s): Black

Mole symbolizes intuition, sensitivity to energy, and trusting in what you feel. Moles have tiny eyes and poor eyesight but aren't blind, as is commonly believed. Because mole is attuned to earth energy, its appearance means that you should deepen your connection to the earth. Take time to dig in the dirt through gardening or landscaping. Feel the consistency, moisture levels, and notice the bits of rock or other things that you find inside. Touch is important to you when mole is around, so give more hugs. You may find that you develop the gift of psychometry at this time. You instantly know information about things simply by touching them. Your psychic abilities are on the rise, so take care when touching other people. If you don't want to accidentally read them, then block your abilities prior to touching them.

Mole is a clever creature and can help you get out of uncomfortable situations with ease. It also helps you uncover hidden information. Mole means that all of your intuitive abilities are on the rise and you are very accurate in your readings. Mole urges you to get outside in nature instead of staying in the house.

Monkey

Element(s): Air, earth | Primary Color(s): Black, brown

Monkey appears when you need to figure something out. Monkey enjoys a good puzzle and its insightfulness can help you get to the root of problems. It means to take action instead of sitting back and waiting for something to happen. Monkey urges you to play and have fun. If you enjoy tricking or pulling practical jokes on people, monkey warns to be careful in your actions. Not everyone enjoys being the brunt of such jokes and may react in anger or a manner you're not expecting. What you mean in good fun they may not take as such.

Monkey encourages you to be resourceful. You can find a solution if you try instead of waiting to be told how to do something. You're very flexible and nimble. You can swiftly move from one situation to another without an interruption in your focus. Grooming is an integral part of monkey's daily life. This means you may need to pay more attention to your appearance. Monkey assists when you need nurturing or the companionship of family and friends. Monkey encourages you to play more and not take life so seriously. Monkey warns against swinging from place to place without focus.

Moose

Element(s): Earth, water | Primary Color(s): Black, brown, gray (in winter)

Moose symbolizes blending in and not attracting attention to yourself. Moose prefers to go unnoticed and likes to be left alone. You tend to have the same qualities, and, like moose, people often underestimate your strength. Moose has huge antlers, which are indicative of great spirituality. At one with itself and nature, moose is deeply connected to the earth. You are grounded as well. Moose warns that you need to camouflage yourself at this time. Stay out of the forefront and in the background. Your time to step to the forefront will happen in due time.

Moose appears when you're embracing your own self-expression. Moose has a unique set of antlers that sets it apart from other animals. This means that you need to search inside to find the qualities that set you apart from other people. Take time to enjoy a stream, sit by a lake, or take a warm bath to reestablish your water connection. Moose is very inconsistent and warns of you being the same. Moose holds the knowledge of the ancients within its being. This knowledge is also within you, and moose can help you access it.

Mosquito

Element(s): Air | Primary Color(s): Black

Mosquito symbolizes travel, survival, and lightness of being. When mosquito shows up, it means that you'll embark on a trip in the near future. This will be a fun and happy time, a joyous occasion. Someone in your family could be getting married or a new baby could be born. The event is filled with positive energy. Mosquito also means that you have high ideals. You can be too blunt when expressing these ideals, which can offend others who do not share the same beliefs. You find yourself in survival mode and fending off attacks from others because of these beliefs.

Mosquito warns against using others to make yourself seem more than what you are or drawing from another's energy to pump up your own self-esteem. It is also a sign to see if anyone is drawing from your reserves without your knowledge. Mosquito means to be assertive but not a pest, to be persistent but not a know it all, to be in control but not controlling. Mosquito can help you transform your attitude, trust your intuition, and revitalize your mind, body, and spirit. Mosquito warns not to let the little things irritate or annoy you.

❧

When combined with our

own unique frequencies,

we can communicate with

and understand the reason

for the animal's presence.

Moth

Element(s): Air | Primary Color(s): Many colors and patterns

Moth symbolizes transformation, finding light in the darkness, and hiding in plain sight. Moth moves through various stages before becoming a winged being. This means you are going through your own transformation at this time. Like moth, it is easy for you to hide in plain sight. You may think you're invisible sometimes because people forget that you're around. There are times when this serves you well, so don't think of it as a negative quality.

Moth means you have phenomenal hearing and can understand even the smallest whisper, and you have learned many secrets this way. You're a night person, just like moth, and do some of your best work when everyone else is sleeping. When you do sleep, make sure you're paying attention to your dreams. Important messages will be relayed to you in them. You're optimistic, give great advice, and are popular. Moth draws others to you. It enhances your intuition and can help you move into a place of positivity and light. Moth warns that something could be eating away at you, like moth eats away at clothing, so it's better to bring it to the light and address it than to keep it in darkness.

Mouse

Element(s): Earth | Primary Color(s): Black, brown,
gray, silver, white

Mouse symbolizes scrutiny, discovery, wisdom, and sensitivity. Mouse has a quiet, nervous nature, is a dependable worker, and prefers sticking with routine. When mouse appears, it's a sign to tone down the excitement in your life, pay attention to details, and stop wasting energy. You're approaching an upcoming change that needs to be handled with delicacy and finesse. Mouse loves exploration but stays close to home. It will only travel twenty feet from its nest and tends to stick to the same paths. This means that sometimes you have to force yourself out of your comfort zone to have adventures and experience new areas.

Mouse is very fertile. This is a sign that your endeavors will be very fertile and productive at this time. If mouse appears, look for new projects or businesses to start. Mouse assists when you need to be organized and pay attention to details. It can help you see important things you may be missing, help you scrutinize the specifics, and let go of whatever isn't needed. It can also help you see the big picture when you become so focused on the details that you forget the ultimate plan.

Narwhal

Element(s): Water | Primary Color(s): Blue-gray at birth, blue-black as juveniles, mottled-gray as adults, all white when elderly

When narwhal appears, it means you need to find balance in your life. You're creative, have an overabundance of ideas, and have the drive to see them to fruition. Your brain never seems to slow down, even in your sleep. Finding balance is important right now. Without balance, you can burn out or get sick because you're wearing yourself out. Narwhal helps you to quiet your mind and make specific plans to ensure success with clear focus while getting the rest you need.

Narwhal means you are always trying to understand yourself. You're interested in a wide range of subject matter, research, and applying the things you learn for self-analysis. Narwhal helps you find purpose in all that you do. You go the extra mile with passion and purpose to learn your own lessons in life and to help others learn their lessons. You may move from job to job or relationship to relationship often, but when you finally settle down, it is with the knowledge that you learned something from every experience. Narwhal assists when you need to complete a project fast.

Octopus (Squid)

Element(s): Water | Primary Color(s): It changes color depending on the environment

When octopus appears, it means to take cover and blend into your surroundings because a threat is near. Octopus ink acts as a cover so it can get away and hide when threatened. Octopus ink is extremely harmful. It can attack the predator's senses of sight, smell, and taste. If octopus gets caught in its own ink, it can die. This means you have to be cautious when instigating an attack on someone because you might just get caught up in your own darkness if there are lies hidden underneath.

Octopus appears when something is holding you back from forward motion. It can allow you to see what is restraining you, whether it's a relationship, job, or your own fears. Once you let go, you'll be able to float freely through an ocean of opportunity and select a new, exciting prospect that allows personal or spiritual growth. When you encounter obstacles, octopus encourages you to just glide right over them and wiggle free from predicaments or uncomfortable situations. Octopus can help you reach out and grab what you want.

Opossum

Element(s): Earth | Primary Color(s): Gray, white

When opossum appears, it means to check your appearance. Not only how you look, but how others perceive your personality, moral code, and character traits. While you aren't particularly concerned about impressing others, knowing their opinions can help you see areas where you can make improvements if you choose to create changes. Opossum means a strong love of family and devotion to those in your close circle of friends. Its pouch symbolizes nurturing, the closeness of loved ones, and hidden resources. This means you tend to always have something up your sleeve, a hidden surprise that can help you out of a jam. Opossum isn't easily intimidated by others higher up in the chain of command.

Opossum has natural acting ability. This serves you well when you don't want others to see your true feelings or if you're going through a personal trauma that you want to hide from the world. Opossum assists when you need a strategy. It is creative and intelligent. It means you can plan a course of action, set that action into motion, and then go after your end goal with the strength of being needed to claim your success.

Orangutan

Element(s): Air, earth (rarely) | Primary Color(s): Brown, red

When orangutan appears, it is a sign that your life may feel like it's spinning out of control. Orangutan means you must pay attention to what's going wrong and take charge again to set things right. Orangutan doesn't give up. It has a high level of intelligence and can use tools and solve problems.

Orangutan also means to look upward, raise yourself to higher elevations both in your personal life and in your spiritual outlook. You can reach great heights once you start climbing. Orangutan lives in the tops of trees and rarely goes to the ground. Everything they need to survive is in the treetops. This is a sign that you have everything you need within you already. You just have to access your core spiritual self to see the true essence of your being. Your soul is your home and you are at peace there. Get to know your higher self better. Orangutan means you need some time alone. Solitude is enlightening. Orangutan can help you reach your goals quickly and efficiently. It also helps when you're trying to manifest your desires into your life.

Ostrich

Element(s): Earth | Primary Color(s): Black, white

Ostrich symbolizes being grounded, connected to the earth, and practical. Ostrich is a bird that can't fly but can run at speeds faster than 40 mph, which means that you are a rational and logical thinker who takes swift action when needed. You may enjoy running as a sport. Not one prone to daydreaming, you work diligently and in a commonsense manner to get the most accomplished in the shortest amount of time. Ostrich lays its eggs in a hole in the ground and sticks its head in several times a day to turn the eggs. While it may appear that ostrich is burying its head in the sand (which is a myth), it is caring for its unborn young.

Ostrich means protection from negative energy, so if you have people around you who are being less than positive, ask ostrich for assistance. When ostrich shows up it means that you need to clean house. Let go of anything that you no longer need, donate it or give it away. When you release clutter, you free up the energy to move easily through your space. In addition to clearing physical clutter, also let go of any emotional or mental clutter that is keeping you bogged down.

Otter

Element(s): Earth, water | Primary Color(s): Brown

Otter symbolizes creativity, imagination, playfulness, and good fortune. When otter appears, it means that you need to take a break from the stress of work and find time to let your curiosity run free. This is a time of exploration and healing, of letting go and having faith that taking a break isn't going to throw everything off track. Joy, happiness, and laughter surround otter. Spending time with family and friends is called for now instead of putting all your focus on work-related deadlines.

Otter means that you're happy with your own success but you're even happier with the success of others. It makes your heart feel bright and lively to see those you care about succeed. This is a good time to start a new business or expand a current one. When otter is around, you might be a bit more emotional than usual and find yourself crying more often. These are usually tears of joy or that show the compassionate side of your nature. Otter also means to get back to the water for balance and to bring out your playful side. Otter also guides you with its curiosity, faith, and love of learning.

Owl

Element(s): Air | Primary Color(s): Black, brown, white

When owl appears, it means you should pay attention to everything around you. Not only what you can see but what you hear and what you intuitively know or feel. There are great important changes coming your way and you need to be aware and prepared to accept them. Be silent and observe. Anything hidden will be revealed at this time.

Owl means you can see the truth behind the disguise, the intention behind the actions, the unexplained within reality. In many traditions, owl is the messenger of death. This doesn't mean a physical death but is symbolic of a major life disruption, transition, or other change. Maybe you're getting married or having a child or moving to a new country. This symbolic death is often very positive.

Owl is also connected to the wisdom of the ages. It seeks knowledge through its keen observation skills. You too glean your knowledge by observing, reading, and absorbing everything you can to give you that same wisdom. You are insightful and tend to know just the right thing to say to open someone's eyes to other possibilities. When owl appears, it often means something big is about to happen to you.

Oyster

Element(s): Water | Primary Color(s): Gray, white

Oyster symbolizes connecting to your inner essence, balance, and peace. When oyster appears, it means you might have to shut down and retreat into your shell to protect yourself. You need to keep quiet, filter out the good from the bad, or put a lid on your emotions until the threat has moved on. Oyster can retain toxins within its body so it's important for you to make sure you're eating healthy and drinking plenty of fluids at this time. It's also important to let go of any negativity that comes your way instead of letting it affect you.

Like the oyster, you're sensitive to your environment. Take a look around. Is there anything you can change to make your work or living area more positive, energetic, or calming? Oysters are difficult to open, and this teaches you that no outside force can change who you truly are on the inside. You don't have to give in to peer pressure but can simply be yourself. Struggles become victories with oyster's assistance. You have the strength within to handle anything that comes your way. Oyster can help you find harmony in mind, body, and spirit.

Panda

Element(s): Air, earth, water | Primary Color(s): Black, red, white

When panda shows up, it means to slow down. You're moving at too fast of a pace and need to take more time to achieve your goals. If you try to force things to happen quickly, you may not get the desired outcome. Panda doesn't hurry through life; instead it enjoys itself along the way. This means you also have to take time to enjoy life, especially if you've been pushing yourself really hard for a long time. Stop, breathe, and relax with panda.

You tend to keep your distance at group events or keep others at arm's length. There is fear that if you let others get too close, then you might get hurt. Panda means it's okay to have boundaries, just know when you're extending them so far that you're pushing people away and adjust them accordingly. Assists when you're going through a time of emotional upheaval. Panda is highly sensitive and enjoys peace and quiet. It can also get emotionally stressed out if it's too noisy or chaotic. It moves slowly and likes it when everyone else does, too. Panda can help you get your emotions back under control by teaching you to climb to greater heights to get out of the fray.

Pangolin

Element(s): Earth | Primary Color(s): Multiple shades of brown

Pangolin means watching your words. The pangolin's tongue is almost as long as its body and is used to catch the ants and termites that they eat. This means that you should be aware of the effect that your words have on other people. You may say something innocently but it is taken wrong by someone else. Pangolin is toothless and has to ingest tiny stones to grind up its food. This means you need to be aware of what you're eating and why. This is a good time to add more fiber into your diet.

Pangolin is the only mammal that has scales instead of hair. The extremely sharp scales are made of keratin and cover a hard calcium plate. These scales are so strong it can protect the pangolin from lions and other fierce predators and often cuts them when they attack. This means you keep your own protective armor in place for fear of being emotionally hurt. Pangolin means to search deep within yourself to discover the cause of your fears and address them so you can move forward. Pangolin is illegally hunted, which means to be aware of any illegal activities happening around you and remove yourself from that situation.

Even though spirit animals choose you,
and can be unpredictable in their appearances,
you can still call upon them
in times of need because of the
special energy connection you share.

Parrot (Macaw)

Element(s): Air | Primary Color(s): Blue, green, red, yellow

When parrot appears, it means to take center stage and stand out in the crowd. It also means someone needs your help and understanding. You may be asked to be a mediator between people having a disagreement. Your inner light shines brightly, your personality sparkles, and your smile is infectious. These qualities draw others to you. You are filled with joy and share it with everyone you meet.

Parrot encourages you to take flight and go after your dreams. Parrot is diplomatic and urges you to be tactful. Avoid spreading gossip or hearsay. There are times to talk and times to keep quiet. Be aware and make sure you're not speaking when you should be listening. Parrot also means to listen to yourself. You're great at giving advice to others, but do you listen and take your own advice? Sometimes the only advice you need is your own. Assists when you need an immediate witty response. Have you ever left a conversation and thought, *I should have said ...?* Parrot will give you those power words when you need them. If you need to add more color to your life parrot can guide you.

Partridge (Pheasant)

Element(s): Earth, air | Primary Color(s): Brown

Partridge symbolizes protection, safety, and taking precautions. Partridge tends to be a low-flying bird, which, according to Greek lore, is about Perdix being transformed into a partridge to save him from a deadly fall. This means you take extra precautionary measures just in case. Partridge tends to be a solitary bird. You're a solitary person as well, and if you don't take care of yourself then who will, right?

When partridge appears, it means that you're on a quest for knowledge. You feel it's important to always learn in life and you take your own advice. Partridge is known for stealing the eggs of other birds and for leaving its own eggs behind. This means that you don't keep all of your eggs in one basket and know when to let go of one thing in order to embrace another. This is especially important in business and when you're dealing with other people. If something doesn't seem right in one of your endeavors, you must know when it's time to walk away even if you're giving the situation all that you've got. Partridge means having the wisdom to know when to let go.

Peacock

Element(s): Earth | Primary Color(s): Blue, green, white

Peacock is connected to the spiritual realms. When it shows up, it means you need to delve into learning and understanding more about spirituality, intuition, dreaming, astral projection, transformation, and approaching life from a place of joy and love. As you grow in these areas, your inner light will become brighter and, like the peacock, you will shine in all of your beautiful inner glory.

Peacock is a determined bird, which means you should never give up on any quest you've set out on. You might even have to strut your stuff to get what you want. When it comes to love, peacock makes a copulatory call when it mates. To attract more peahens, peacock fakes the call to make the hens think he's getting busy more often than he really is. That's a pretty creative way to woo the girls. When peacock appears, it means you're being a bit too vain. Turn down the vanity and turn up the modesty to get back in balance. Peacock's call sounds like it is saying *Help! Help! Help!* While it may sound like it's asking for your help, instead it symbolically means help is right here if you need it, just ask peacock for assistance.

Penguin

Element(s): Earth, water | Primary Color(s): Black, blue, white

When penguin appears, it means to develop your spirituality. You're not finished with your spiritual growth, so keep exploring. Meditation and dreaming are two areas where penguin can show you hidden knowledge and open your eyes to new information, enabling you to become more spiritually aware. Penguin is nurturing. This means you care for the young and teach them how to be responsible, independent adults. Penguin doesn't have natural ground predators, so it's not afraid of humans and will approach with interest. This means you aren't a fearful person and have an insatiable curiosity, which can get you into trouble if you're not careful.

Penguin is a flightless bird, which means you're grounded, balanced, secure in yourself, and can dive to tremendous depths to uncover any knowledge you seek. Penguin urges you to investigate new thoughts and ideals. Penguin can help you deal with the effects of any transitions. This means that even if you feel you've been stripped of everything, the situation is temporary and life will return to normal; you just can't give up hope.

Piranha

Element(s): Water | Primary Color(s): Silver

Piranha has a bad rap due to the way it uses its razor-sharp teeth to make a quick meal out of anything that falls into its domain. If you look at the piranha as a spirit animal, you'll see that it is symbolic of teamwork and appreciating what you are given. This means that, like piranha, you work well with a team while supporting the other team members instead of undercutting them. Piranha means you have an *all for one and one for all* attitude. What's good for the group is good for the individual.

Piranha means that you don't take things for granted. When good things fall into your lap, you don't question why you're receiving it, but give thanks for the gift. Piranha doesn't waste anything. This is a sign for you to look at your own actions. If you're being wasteful of food, energy, or your time, make the necessary changes so you waste less. If you're feeling restless and unhappy with your life, piranha can help you see how truly blessed you are. It can help you express your feelings to those who matter, and stand up for yourself when needed. Piranha urges you to seek the company of others, especially when you're feeling lonely.

Platypus

Element(s): Earth, water | Primary Color(s): Brown

Platypus is one of only five species of monotremes, which are mammals that lay eggs instead of having a live birth. This means that you have your own unique way of doing things and that it's easy for you to step outside of society's expectations and do what feels normal and right for you. Platypus means to stay in tune with your own inner self, your higher consciousness, because your purpose is great. You're able to detect what you need through energy and have faith that you're being led in the right direction in life.

Platypus appears when you're confused by something that should have an obvious answer or when you are seeking a deeper and more complete understanding of a situation. If you're being too emotional—overly sad or feel down in the dumps—and can't seem to boost yourself to a higher vibration, call on platypus to push you out of the emotional rut and into the realm of understanding. Forgiveness may be necessary at this time. You may need to forgive yourself or someone else. Platypus is curious, which means that your curiosity could get the best of you right now.

Pond Skater

Element(s): Water | Primary Color(s): Black, brown

Pond skaters are insects that can walk on water. Their appearance means you need to tread lightly at this time. Things are happening behind the scenes of a situation that you're unaware of, so get all the information you can before you say or do anything. Pond skaters stab their prey, which means that your words can have a stabbing, hurtful effect if you're not careful. Pond skaters' legs act as paddles and rudders to move them across the water quickly. You too have the ability to steer yourself in the direction you want and to achieve your goals quickly. The key is not to allow the weight of other people's problems or things that you can't control to push you into the water and slow you down.

Pond skaters can detect even the smallest ripple or vibration in the water. You too are attuned to the frequencies of the people around you and the situations you're involved in. Don't ignore something even if it feels small and insignificant. It may be very important. Pond skaters mean that you are in a time of transformation, so be aware of the things happening around and to you at this time.

Porcupine

Element(s): Earth | Primary Color(s): Black, brown, white

When porcupine appears, it is a warning to stay alert for some type of attack coming your way. This could be in the form of a disgruntled coworker, family member, or even from a business. Porcupine also means to venture out and see the world. Porcupine usually lives alone or in groups of around six. This means that you work best in small groups.

Have you lost your childlike innocence, your sense of awe and wonder? Porcupine can help you get it back when you've become disillusioned with people or the world. Today's world is so hectic and stressful that it's easy to get caught up in the negative and forget to see the beauty of our environment or the love of family and friends because we simply overlook them or take them for granted. Think about how a child is awed at the simplest magic trick when something disappears (behind your back) or when they see something they've never seen before (like rain). Can you see the wonder and magic in life again? Sure you can. Let porcupine lead the way. It assists when someone is giving you a hard time and you need help getting away from them.

Raccoon

Element(s): Earth, water | Primary Color(s): Black, gray

Raccoon symbolizes resourcefulness, intelligence, and communication. When raccoon appears, it means you need to do something constructive with your hands. Any kind of hands-on activity will work. Raccoon is a friendly animal but can react ferociously if threatened. This same quality applies to you. You're outgoing, friendly, and will do anything for anyone, but if someone talks about you behind your back or threatens you in any way, watch out. Your reaction is usually quick, unexpected, and your words will rip through someone. You don't back down from a fight and will attack first if necessary. Raccoon warns not to lose your mind like that. Try to control the reaction and take measured, calculated steps. You'll still get what you want through controlled fierceness without coming across as crazy.

Raccoon warns that it would be easy for you to become obsessed with washing your hands or food so make sure you're staying in balance. Raccoon is ingenious and can figure out original and unique ways to accomplish tasks. Raccoon assists when you need to hide behind a mask of secrecy.

Raven (Crow)

Element(s): Air | Primary Color(s): Black

Raven symbolizes speaking up for yourself, learning new skills, and studying metaphysical topics. Raven's intelligence makes learning fun, and you'll retain the knowledge faster. Raven means there is a situation coming your way where you'll need to voice your feelings instead of holding your tongue. Raven means to be aware of the meanings of dreams and visions. While raven has often been thought to be a dark messenger that foretells death, seeing raven can be a warning instead of meaning death. There may be someone who doesn't have your best interest at heart, or who might betray you or try to deceive you in some way. If raven appears, keep these things in mind, watch what you say, and stay alert to any changes in people's actions or words.

Raven has often been referred to as the "keeper of secrets," which means you've got a secret you must keep either for yourself or for someone else, and it's a doozy. Keep it safe and secure inside you. Raven is metaphysical and symbolizes reaching through the darkness to find and resolve your inner conflicts, then letting your light shine bright. It's healing oneself from within.

Rhinoceros

Element(s): Earth, water | Primary Color(s): Gray

When rhinoceros appears, it means to slow down and be patient. Trying to push or rush a situation will only have adverse effects. It can help you rejuvenate physically, renew your inner self, and heal emotionally. Assists when you need to return to center, remain calm, learn from your higher self, and find balance in your life.

Rhino can help you know yourself better. Rhino urges you to be true to yourself without letting peer pressure or other outside influences sway you from your path. It's important not to rely only on what you see (because appearances can be deceiving) but to instead rely on all of your senses. You are powerful, centered, grounded, and secure in the awareness of your own spirit and universal energy. If you're distracted, worried, out of sorts, or feel like you're sinking into the mud, ask rhino to guide you back to solid ground with its sure-footed strength. It can also help you become thick-skinned so you're no longer upset by other people's actions or words. You see them as they are and maintain harmony within yourself instead of reacting to their drama.

Salamander

Element(s): Earth, water | Primary Color(s): Black, gray,
green, orange, pink, red, yellow, and many other colors
and color combinations

When salamander appears, it means change is coming. This will probably be some type of major change in your life that will create new opportunities and forward motion. But it usually results in the loss of something prior to seeing the opportunity. It's the door closing before the window opens. It's letting go of something holding you back so a new opportunity can come your way. There's only so much room available for the things you can do on the physical realm. When your cup starts overflowing, you either have to make a conscious decision to let something go to free up time and energy so new things will come to you, or the universe will do it for you.

Salamander can guide you through all of the highs and lows as you travel the path of transformation. Salamander can also help in times that aren't a crisis. If you're feeling bored or need a new project to keep you busy, salamander can point you in the right direction. Salamander also has an important role in helping with your spiritual transformation and growth.

Salmon

Element(s): Water | Primary Color(s): Pinkish orange

Salmon symbolizes home, rebirth, and a positive attitude. You may need to let go of something that's holding you back or reconnect to something you've forgotten. Salmon means you're about to go on a grand adventure. Pack your bags and let salmon lead the way. Salmon shows distant travels to faraway lands, but it always returns home to recharge before heading out again. Salmon means that during this journey, whether it's spiritual or personal, you'll discover Divine meaning, purpose, and joy in your life. You're destined to see the universal picture, not just the big one. There is purpose in everything and you're shown how all parts are interconnected.

You're very energetic and often forget to eat because you become immersed in your discoveries or the work you're doing. Salmon gives you determination, confidence, agility, and the ability to understand and share Divine messages, spiritual knowledge, and ancient wisdom. Your insightfulness will be important in helping others understand their own purpose. Assists when you need to be more adventurous or daring. Salmon can help you jump over obstacles to get to your goals.

Scorpion

Element(s): Earth | Primary Color(s): Black, brown, green, red

Scorpion symbolizes control, inner strength, and good defenses. It also symbolizes high sex drive, beauty, and jealousy. Scorpion's elevated sense of vibration alerts it to environmental changes. This means that you're sensitive to your surroundings and use your intuition to sense energy changes in people and places. You're attuned to your own sexuality, see the beauty in everyone, and use your sense of control and inner strength to protect yourself and avoid being jealous.

When scorpion appears, it is a sign to start doing research on a topic that interests you to expand your knowledge. If scorpion appears when you're dieting, it's a sign not to give up. When threatened, scorpion is fast and deadly accurate when delivering its sting. You too are quick-witted and speak with words that can pierce deeply. If you're involved in an altercation, you tend to act first and ask questions later. Scorpion reminds you to protect yourself from those who mean you harm, to follow your own beliefs and convictions, and to always ask for what you want because that's the easiest way to get it.

Sea Horse (Sea Dragon)

Element(s): Water | Primary Color(s): Blue, brown, green, orange, pink, purple, yellow, multicolored

Sea horse symbolizes placidity, gentle movements, slowing down, and enjoying life. It is the power of your subconscious, your higher self. It means you have a unique outlook, which may often be different from those around you. People may tell you one thing but you can see deeper to the heart of the matter.

Sea horse mates for life, and they meet each morning to do a pairing dance, which includes changing colors. This means that you're compatible and giving in relationships. Listen closely when sea horse appears. It can be hard to hear, as if it's whispering to you in a soft voice from a great distance. But its words will be filled with important messages that will help you grow in your personal life or in spirit. Sea horse means to focus and not take anything in your life for granted. It means to let go of anger, fears, and negative emotions; be present; live in the moment; and share joy with those around you. It means someone around you may need your protection or for you to stand up for them in the near future.

Seal (Sea Lion)

Element(s): Earth, water | Primary Color(s): Brown, gray

Seal symbolizes creativity, inspiration, sensitivity, and protection. Seal means you often feel drawn to bodies of water, can undergo a complete transformation in your appearance if you so desire, and are creative in finding ways around situations. When seal appears, it means that while you're agreeable and friendly most of the time, if pushed your words can have a bite. Because of your inner sensitivity, you may often regret any negative things you say and often take steps to make things right with the other person. Your personality is warm, caring, and you're an inspiration to others. You have a protective streak for those you feel close to, for children, for animals, and for those you feel are being wronged in some way.

If seal appears, it means to immerse yourself in your creative talents. Can you compose a song, write a book, or create beautiful pieces of jewelry? You may even choose to pursue a career using your artistic talents. Seal will appear when you've forgotten to be appreciative and joyful. It will show you how to find and express the happiness inside yourself.

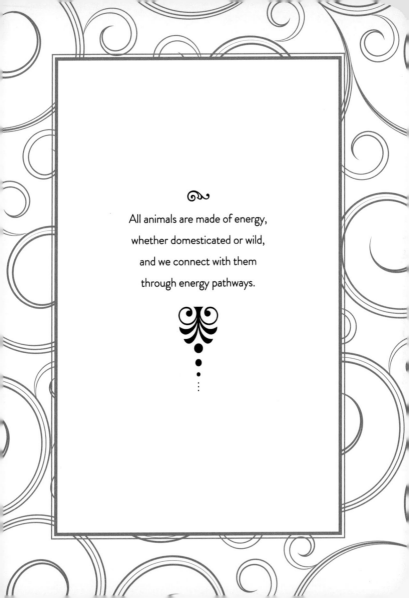

All animals are made of energy,
whether domesticated or wild,
and we connect with them
through energy pathways.

Shark

Element(s): Water | Primary Color(s): Gray, white

Shark symbolizes determination, strength, and speed. Shark means you are a go-getter who knows what you want and will go after it full speed ahead. You're not afraid of competition and know when to make a lightning-fast move or when to hang back and wait for the perfect opportunity. When shark appears, it means that you need to look at your behavior. Are you acting in an unprincipled, devious, or ruthless way to get what you want? If so, shark's message is to take it easy, regroup, and scope out the situation using tact and skill.

Shark also means to increase your activity level. If you're not getting enough exercise, you can become agitated and frenzied, taking out your frustrations on others. Shark warns against becoming a workaholic and not taking time to swim just for fun. Shark will swim in naturally slow patterns when it's happy and comfortable. This is a sign to slow down, leave the anxiousness behind, and regroup. Shark's powerful and sometimes ferocious nature is a warning that you need to remain alert for threats so you can protect yourself. It assists when you're stuck in an emotional rut and can't find your way.

Shrimp

Element(s): Water | Primary Color(s): Pink

Shrimp symbolizes responsibility, communication, and being fully aware. When shrimp shows up, get ready to give advice to help someone younger than yourself. Shrimp means taking on a sudden responsibility that you weren't expecting to have to shoulder. It means getting through to someone who is blocking everyone who is trying to help them. Shrimp gives you the ability to see in poor conditions and to see through someone's mask that hides their pain.

Shrimp makes you strong and able to handle vulnerabilities of others and that you have within yourself. Shrimp warns against striking out suddenly and urges you to control your anger. Understanding is of the utmost importance at this time. Shrimp is grounding and keeps you balanced. Its keen eyesight helps you to see the truth of matters. Shrimp helps you to get over fear by pushing it backward so you can move forward. It helps you go with the flow of life, taking things as they happen. While you may be shy and prefer not to be the center of attention, you have no problem stepping up to the plate and putting yourself out there if you're needed.

Silverfish

Element(s): Earth | Primary Color(s): Silver

Silverfish symbolizes a connection to ancient knowledge, health, and longevity. Silverfish have been around for more than 400 million years. They can go a year without eating, which can account for their ability to live up to eight years, which is a long time for a bug. Their diet primarily consists of sugars, starches, and carbohydrates, which means that you need to watch how much of these items you're including in your own diet. If you're trying to lose weight, then silverfish warns to cut back on these types of foods. They hate the smell of citrus, so that means you should add more fruits to your diet.

Silverfish as associated with filthy conditions, so if you're seeing silverfish, the message could be that it's time to do some spring cleaning. You may also need to pay better attention to your personal hygiene. If you've been putting off going to the dentist or getting a haircut, make the appointment soon. Silverfish can run very fast and can jump up to two feet. This means that it's a good time to start a new exercise program to go along with your dietary changes.

Skunk

Element(s): Earth | Primary Color(s): Black, white

When skunk appears, it means to examine the way you're dealing with others, stop taking yourself too seriously, and lighten up. This means you have to make sure you're not coming across as defensive without reason, arrogant, or reclusive. Skunk encourages you to be adventurous, curious, adaptable, inquisitive, playful, and loving. You're not easily intimidated and are courageous but not aggressive. Skunk means to begin a new adventure. Take a trip, start a new project, or become an authority on a new subject. Skunk encourages you to keep learning, investigating, and uncovering interesting things in your life.

Skunk shows up when you need to have a calm confidence but feel like a nervous wreck. It will calm you and guide you through turmoil. Assists when you need to stop letting others intimidate or push you around. If you're involved in a situation where someone is taking advantage of you, it might be hard for you to take the first step to defend yourself because of your kind, loving, gentle, and shy nature. Right now you need to step out of your comfort zone and stand up for yourself.

Sloth

Element(s): Air, earth, water | Primary Color(s): Brown, gray, green (when algae is present)

Sloth symbolizes slowing down, making steady progress, and never giving up on your dreams. When sloth appears, it means you need to go at your own pace and take your time to accomplish your goals. You're very aware of others and the way they perceive you. They may think you'll be easy to take advantage of just because your natural pace is more laid back than their own. You're quite capable of protecting yourself against threatening aggressors.

Sloth assists when you need to tap into and hone your intuitive gifts. You tend to have clairvoyant visions, but sometimes you don't know how to interpret them. Sloth gives you clear vision so you can see the event unfold and the perception to understand the meanings behind what you see. If you feel as if you're on a speeding train and can't keep up with your own life, sloth can help you slow down the pace so it's easier to manage. Sloth can help you look at life or specific situations from a unique perspective. When you look from a different angle, you may be surprised at what is revealed.

Snail

Element(s): Earth | Primary Color(s): Brown, tan

Snail symbolizes patience. When snail shows up, it means to leave behind everything you thought about being patient. You are about to experience a situation where you'll feel your patience is being stretched so thin that it will break. Just hang in there because snail also gives you the ability to see the end results long before you get there. Everything will work out as it should, and your patience will prove the best path to have taken in the end.

Snail means that you're protected from negativity. You are always aware of what's happening around you. While you're not paranoid, you're usually on guard, so that you're never caught unaware. Snail means that you're a loner who avoids crowds. This is because you're attuned to energy and too much can have an overwhelming effect on you. This is a good time to practice raising your frequency so that you don't feel out of place if there are people around. When snail shows up, it means that you need to trust in others, which is hard for you to do, but know that with trust comes balance, which you need at this time.

Snake (Viper)

Element(s): Air, earth, water | Primary Color(s): Black, green, orange, yellow, or any color or any combination of colors

Snake symbolizes transformation, awakening of creative forces, and connection to higher consciousness. When snake appears, it means you're coming into a time of extreme spiritual growth, and you'll become more connected to the energy of the universe. You will experience a surge in all areas of your life during this period of spiritual growth. Your intuition will become more accurate, your dreams may become prophetic, and you'll know more than ever before.

Snake indicates that you'll be offered new opportunities, you'll become more ambitious, and you'll experience a metamorphosis at every turn. Snake is your protector as you grow and change. Snake's eyes are always open and protected by an opaque scale, which means that during this phase of your life, you will see more than you ever expected to see. With this sight comes an internal understanding without explanation. You just know things without being told. You're alert to everything happening around you and are embracing the surge in spirituality that you're experiencing.

Sparrow

Element(s): Earth | Primary Color(s): Brown

Sparrow symbolizes community, friendliness, and productivity. When sparrow shows up, it means you'll be involved in a group project or you're going to be spending a lot of time hanging out with your friends or with a group of people. To sparrow there is safety in numbers, because they are a small bird, they do everything together in groups and are happy to be part of that group instead of alone. Sparrow means that you're entering a very productive time of your life and that any ventures you start now, especially if they involve a group of people in some way, will be successful.

Sparrow is connected to the Divine, higher thoughts, and ideals. This means that you're striving to connect to your own spiritual self at a higher level. Sparrow's small size means that you don't have to do big things to make a difference in your own life or someone else's life. Sometimes the little things mean so much more. Sparrow encourages you to keep your self-esteem high because you can do anything you set your mind to do, even if others tell you that your dreams are impossible. They're not and you will achieve them with sparrow by your side.

Spider

Element(s): Air, earth | Primary Color(s): Black, brown, yellow,
plus every other color

Spider symbolizes creativity, patience, and resourceful-ness. When spider appears, it means to begin a new cre-ative project. Spider means receptivity, and if you were to start a new business that embraces your creative talents it will be successful. Spider helps you get in tune with the flow of life around you. Spider has an intuitive knack for being at the right place at the right time. This enables you to achieve success in your business ventures.

Spider warns not to get caught up in a web of lies. Lis-ten closely and use your intuition to connect to the truth under the words. By being aware, you can avoid prob-lems. This also means not to create your own deceitful web by presenting yourself as more than you are or by making promises you can't keep. Be honest and truthful in all areas of your life to make the speediest progress to your ultimate goals. Lies, deceit, and misrepresentation will ultimately catch up with you, so move forward in truth and honesty. Spider assists when you need to get rid of toxic people in your life.

Starfish

Element(s): Water | Primary Color(s): Blue, orange, pink, purple,
red, yellow, and many mixed colors and patterns

Starfish symbolizes hope, courage, and confidence. Starfish means you don't let opportunities pass you by, instead you reach out and grab them with both hands and hold on tight. When starfish appears, it means you are looking at life in black and white instead of seeing the colors around you. You may be taking things too seriously when they're meant in fun. Surround yourself with people with colorful personalities. You have a lot of confidence that you will excel in whatever task you undertake.

Starfish also reminds you not to be too controlling with people. It's your nature to pry things open but sometimes you have to let others open up to you instead of forcing them to let you see inside. Use finesse when interacting with others. Starfish assists when you need to start over. When you need to begin again, starfish can guide you as you rebuild your life and replace anything you've lost. Just like starfish, you may not see it well at the time but it will make itself known one day. Like starfish, you are unique, inspiring, and beautiful.

Stick Insect

Element(s): Earth | Primary Color(s): Black, brown, green

Stick insect symbolizes blending into your environment, being independently productive, and being tactically creative. Stick insect appears when you need to build up your defenses. It has a rather weak first line of defense. It doesn't bite but will use its sharp leg spines to inflict pain. Stick insect shows you the power in stillness. By staying still, watching, and waiting, you will know the course of action you should take. You are extraordinary and people respect the uniqueness within you.

Stick insect warns to not live in the past, which can cause problems dealing with current situations. Let the past go to experience forward motion. Stick insect assists when you need to have the element of surprise on your side. If you're trying to surprise someone, follow the lead of stick insect by doing the unexpected. Stick insect can also help you keep things hidden. Stick insect urges you to not keep all of your eggs in one basket. Scatter things around because you never know what will be picked up and nurtured until it grows to fruition. You have many great ideas. It's impressive how much you can accomplish in one day.

Stingray

Element(s): Water | Primary Color(s): Black, white

Stingray symbolizes steadiness under pressure, persistent movement, and forward navigation. When stingray appears, it means you're able to blend in. Regardless of the situation, you are able to hide in plain sight and often go unnoticed. This is fine with you because you can find out the scoop about things going on around you. Like the stingray, you are graceful and move with elegance. You have a refined presence and people look up to you. You listen to your higher self and follow your inner guidance. You're very aware; not much gets by you.

Stingray's sense of touch is heightened, which means you may have heightened intuition especially in psychometry or as an empath. This is a time to stay focused and keep distractions to a minimum. You need to hunker down and get things done instead of procrastinating and putting it off. You've worked hard to get where you are, so don't move backward when you still need to be moving forward unless the step back is absolutely necessary for forward progress. Soon you'll be able to lie down and rest, just not yet. Stingray assists when you aren't sure what direction to take.

It is truly a gift
from the animal
to be able to share
their frequency.

Stink Bug

Element(s): Air, earth | Primary Color(s): Green

Stink bug means heightened intuition and being able to see synchronicities in unrelated events in order to understand the bigger picture of your life. When stink bug is around, it means you're transforming and growing in your own spirituality. Stink bug's scent means that you're protecting yourself, but you need to examine this because you may not need protection but instead need guidance.

Stink bug can help you understand the meaning of your dreams. It encourages you to look at every aspect of your thoughts, visions, and dreams to glean a greater understanding of the course you should take in a situation. Everything goes together, there is a connection to all that is within the universe, and it's up to you to find that connection and implement it in your life. This is a time of learning about yourself spiritually, of understanding your purpose. Stink bug brings about change. This can be a change in your way of thinking, your character, or your actions. It can help you see clearly and let go of any fear that is holding you back. Now is a time to right past wrongs and to move forward on your path.

Swan

Element(s): Earth, water | Primary Color(s): Black, white

Swan symbolizes love, fidelity, and romance. Swans mate for life, yet each remains a unique individual. When swan appears, it means there is a new relationship coming into your life. You will meet someone new at work, make a new friend, or start a new love relationship. Swan means to look at inner beauty, not just someone's outer appearance. When it comes to any relationship, you have an intuitive knowledge of the other person and understand their emotions and the way they think. This makes you an easy person to work with and a likely confidant.

You're loyal and once you're committed to someone, you're committed for life. Even if you go your separate ways, if that person ever comes to you for help in the future, you'll be there for them. Swan reminds you to express yourself with clarity, to take time out of every day for silence, and to always hum or whistle a little tune at some point during your day. This will give you a sense of balance and keep you connected with your inner self. Assists when you need to have faith, see the mysteries in life, and reconnect with your bliss.

Swordfish

Element(s): Water | Primary Color(s): Black, dark blue, silver

Swordfish symbolizes adventure and independence. It is known for its long, swordlike bill. It instills a sense of swashbuckling action, risk-taking, and entitlement. Its physical power and uniqueness makes it command attention. You also have the ability to grab the attention of others because of your unique appearance or skills.

When swordfish appears, it means to live life to its fullest. You're an energetic, proud, but sometimes eccentric person who has big ideas and dreams and you aren't afraid to go out and grab them. You're highly intelligent, adventurous, and work extremely well under pressure. You have a positive and happy outlook on life and are able to infuse those feelings into others with your outgoing energy and bubbling personality. Swordfish can take giant leaps out of the water, which indicates that you are willing to expose your inner self to others in order to spread positivity in life. You have a lot going for you, things seem to always work in your favor or you're at the right place at the right time. Swordfish assists when you need to win.

Tarantula

Element(s): Earth | Primary Color(s): Brown

Tarantula symbolizes perfect timing, stealth, and longevity. It means you know when to wait, when to use stealth to sneak up on your competition or to find out secret information, and when to pounce. When tarantula shows up it means to make use of what you have in creative ways. While tarantulas don't spin webs like most spiders, they do use their silk to strengthen the walls in their burrows or to wrap up their eggs. What talents do you have that you can put to a unique use?

Female tarantulas can live more than thirty years in the wild. This means to take your time and do things right the first time so you don't have to do it over later. Tarantula means creating your own path, following your own dreams, and staying grounded in reality as you reach for what you desire. It means not letting others intimidate you along the path. With patience you will achieve your dreams. Because of their large size, eight legs, and hairy body, tarantulas are pretty scary looking when in fact their bite is no worse than a bee sting. Tarantula means that appearances can be deceiving, so you should always look for the truth underneath.

Tasmanian Devil

Element(s): Earth | Primary Color(s): Black

Tasmanian devil means aggression, self-defense, and protection. The Tasmanian devil is a fearsome predator. When it shows up it means you're having a difficult time dealing with anger, rage, or violent emotions. Tasmanian devil can help you get these emotions under control. If you feel you've been betrayed and can't find it in your heart to forgive the person, Tasmanian devil will show you the way. It will fill you with confidence and courage and will allow you to see the situation from a different point of view so that you let go of the negativity you've been holding on to.

Tasmanian devil is a warning to watch out for your own health. Don't let illness go untreated or a cold could become raging bronchitis. Be proactive in regard to your health and remember that negative emotions can cause illness, so don't hold them inside. You might find your-self in a situation where you have to defend yourself or protect someone else. Tasmanian devil by your side will make the other person wish they'd just left you alone. Tasmanian devil urges you to be honest with yourself and the people around you.

Termite

Element(s): Earth | Primary Color(s): White

Termite symbolizes building, social interaction, and cooperation. Some species of termite can build huge mounds that act like a ventilation system over their underground nests. This means that you're an excellent builder and can see intricate designs. You'd excel in a career in architecture, interior design, or any type of construction. Termite means that you'll work until you drop. When you're focused on something or on a deadline, nothing else matters until the job is complete. This extreme focus and ability to work fast under a deadline makes you a valuable employee. However, more often than not, you own the business.

Termite means that you enjoy working in groups and are a good team player. You don't have an over-inflated ego. Termite means to look around for someone who might be playing you and trying to upset the balance in your life. While termite builds, it also destroys, so it's important to look for weakness in your life. Where can you reinforce the structure of your life to keep the foundations solid and stable? Termite means that someone is out to undermine you, so be aware.

Tick

Element(s): Earth | Primary Color(s): Brown

Tick means to be persistent in your pursuits. Tick is a determined pest, one that can hide away without you knowing that you've become its host. When tick shows up, it means that you'll be successful, but you need to keep things quiet until your goal is met. Silence is golden so that others don't take advantage of you or spoil your plans. Don't share your ideas at this time. Keep your own secrets so others aren't able to benefit from your hard work without your permission. Tick also means to make sure you're not taking advantage of others without realizing it.

Tick means you are putting on a tough facade out of the fear of being hurt. Tick warns against getting stuck in a routine and encourages you to add variety to your life. Tick exists on blood, which is a sign to change up the kinds of food that you eat. Tick means that you're going to experience obstacles and that you'll be involved with situations or people who you believe are pests, but instead of letting yourself get freaked out or annoyed, trust in your ability to climb to great heights.

Tiger

Element(s): Earth, water | Primary Color(s): Black, orange, white

Tiger symbolizes strength, beauty, and uniqueness. Its stripes are also patterned in its skin, so if you were to shave a tiger, it would still have stripes. This means you are a distinctive, one of a kind, beautiful individual with an incredible amount of strength and willpower. Tiger has round pupils, sees in color, and appears when you need to see the true colors of someone. This means you're able to see with more perception than most. You trust your instincts. You're a strong leader, exceptional business person, and often run your own company. While you don't have any problems delegating tasks, the ultimate control stays with you. When you see something you want, you go after it with all you've got.

Tiger means that others see you as sexy and passionate. You're a big flirt and go out of your way to make others feel better about themselves, but you never lead someone on if you have no intention of following through. Tiger loves to swim, which means you're probably drawn to water activities. It assists when you need to make plans and carry them out. Tiger gives you the courage to stay the path.

Toucan

Element(s): Air | Primary Color(s): Black, green, orange, yellow

Toucan is symbolic of communicating in a direct, clear, and concise manner. It means to get your point across using bold, colorful adjectives that encourage others. Toucan means you are a leader who is motivational and inspiring. If you need to add flair to your wardrobe, your home, or your work environment, ask toucan for assistance. Toucan can help you get in touch with your higher self and increase your ability to draw your own inspiration from universal consciousness. It is strength when you need it and courage when you feel you might fail. It pushes fear aside so that you can shine.

Toucan is a colorful showman that gives you its brilliance when you must perform or speak in front of others. It means that you're a true friend, caring, and will go out of your way to help someone even if they say they're fine. You know the truth and go the extra mile. When toucan shows up, it means to add more fruits and nuts to your diet. Toucan urges you to be bold and vivacious while living life to the fullest. Find your joy, happiness, and inner peace with toucan as your guide.

Trout

Element(s): Water | Primary Color(s): Brown, red, tan, yellow

Trout means forward movement toward a goal or on your spiritual path. Trout means listening to your own truth and not letting others force their will upon you. If you find yourself in a difficult situation, then you may need to gain a clearer understanding of all of the undercurrents happening around you. Trout urges you to say what you mean and mean what you say. Don't tell lies or enhance a situation to make yourself look better. Be bold, forthright, and truthful in all that you do to keep the waters clear instead of muddied.

Trout is indicative of having a strong self-esteem, of knowing what you want and then going out and getting it. It means having strong decision-making abilities and not doubting yourself. You can be very successful as an entrepreneur if trout is guiding you. Trout warns not to think so highly of yourself that you become arrogant or stubborn about change. Water is always flowing, always changing. If you don't flow and change with your environment and the people around you, then you could get left behind. Trout is a sign that good things are coming your way, so be ready for surprises.

Turtle

Element(s): Earth, water | Primary Color(s): Brown, green

When turtle appears, it means you're moving too fast. Connect with the creativeness of your inner self and your core soul truths. Turtle reminds you that slow and steady wins the race. Turtle also teaches the importance of being balanced and grounded. If turtle is out of balance, it can tip over onto its back and can die if it doesn't flip back to its stomach. This means you need to always head in the right direction. If you get turned around, set yourself back on course as soon as possible.

Turtle is persistent and determined. It doesn't give up and neither do you. Turtle is also connected to ancient wisdom, which means that deep within your shell, you know the answers you seek. In this lifetime, part of your path is to accept that which cannot be seen so you can do what must be done. Success awaits; take your time getting there. Turtle also means it's time to trust in the knowledge within you, be particularly attentive of how you're navigating your life, and shelter those you love or who are important to you. Turtle assists when you are engaged in a task that requires attention to details.

Vulture (Buzzard)

Element(s): Air, earth | Primary Color(s): Black, brown, gray, white

Vulture symbolizes life cycles, renewal, and cleansing. When vulture appears, it means it's time to equalize things in your life. Vulture means to look past outward appearances in order to see the unique individual inside. There's a story that when the sun got too close to earth, vulture pushed it away using its head and mighty wings. The feathers were burned off of his head as he saved the world. This story means that someone can have great strength of character inside and reasons for their outward appearance. If you don't take the time to know others, then you're missing out on the possibility of making a wonderful new friend.

Vulture is an expert in cleanliness. When it appears, it means to remove all of the clutter from your home and work environment, let go of all the excess baggage in your personal life, and let go of any clutter in your mind that is causing you excessive stress. Vulture enables you to see the good in people, make the best out of a difficult situation, and encourages you to always look for the silver lining. It assists when you need purity of mind, body, and spirit.

Walrus

Element(s): Earth, water | Primary Color(s): Brown

Walrus is thought to be the keeper of knowledge, which means its message is for you to undertake higher learning. This could be enrolling in college or taking some night classes. It could even be just learning on your own through reading as many books on as many topics that interest you as you can. Walrus is the teacher when you're ready to become the student. It encourages you to find others who share your same interests and to become part of a group. From the group setting you will learn even more due to the varying opinions of the other members.

Walrus encourages you to expand your horizons to see far beyond where your physical vision ends and to enter the area of the Divine. Now is the time to ask lots of questions. If you're progressing along your spiritual path, you'll discover that just as walrus showed up to guide you, other teachers will show up to help you expand your consciousness. Walrus reminds you to stay stable and grounded as you reach greater levels of enlightenment. This is also a time to keep yourself protected from influences who may not have your best interest at heart.

Warthog

Element(s): Earth | Primary Color(s): Brown, black, gray

Warthog means to keep your friends close and your enemies closer. Warthog is peaceful but will fight a strong battle if provoked. It will die to ensure the safety of its family. You are in a role of protector when warthog shows up. You're vigilant and quick to sense if danger is near. You're extremely protective of your children in your care.

Warthog means you're very intuitive and observant. Not much gets by you. If someone is using you, they may think they've hidden their real intention but you see right through them. You can also see the strengths in people when they may not realize them yet. This makes you an exceptional boss who gives people the opportunity to move upward. Warthog means you're a warrior and will take on any task, no matter how difficult it may seem or if there is a chance you could be hurt in the process. Some battles are worth the fight and warthog does love to take on a challenge. Warthog can help you if you're unsure if a person is trustworthy or not. Warthog means to have fun in life, to enjoy all that you do, and take nothing for granted.

Wasp

Element(s): Air | Primary Color(s): Black, brown, yellow

Wasp means to make your dreams reality. Wasp symbolizes development, implementation of an idea, and productivity in developing it into reality. Wasp is symbolic of new beginnings. It's a social creature that works well in a group. Wasp means that if you've ever wanted to build something, now is the time to do it. This could be a home, a business, or a friendship. Put in the work now to reap the rewards of your labor later. Wasp is also symbolic of fertility so if you've been thinking of starting a business or a family then it's a good time to start in order to find success.

Wasp means that while you work well in a group, you aren't dependent on that group for your livelihood. Wasp means you think things through before undertaking a task instead of just jumping in headfirst without any planning. Wasp means you like organization and order. If things are a mess, you're the person others ask to fix it and get everything running smoothly and in an organized manner again. People look up to you because they feel they can talk to you but they also know that your words can sting. Wasp means you're passionate, hungry for success, and willing to go the extra mile to achieve it.

Weasel (Marten, Mink)

Element(s): Earth, water | Primary Color(s): Brown, white

Weasel symbolizes keeping secrets, fast action, and expressing joy. Weasel means to stop, look, and listen. There is something going on that you're unaware of and you need to be very observant to uncover the truth in case there is someone planning an attack. You also may be in a situation where you'll have to be on guard, so proceed with caution.

Weasel means that if you need to speak up, you do so without hesitation and often take the lead. But there are also times when you are so silent people forget you're there. This enables you to obtain information you may otherwise not have heard but will benefit your path to achieving your goal. You tend to like your solitude as much as weasel does. Weasel can also spray a nasty, stinking fluid like a skunk when it feels threatened, which means you also have tricks that will take your competition unawares. Weasel assists when you're feeling trapped, suspicious, or as if you're being pushed to do something that you don't want to do, weasel can help you maneuver out of the situation and turn it around to your advantage.

Whale

Element(s): Water | Primary Color(s): Black, blue, brown, gray, white

Whale symbolizes the power of vibrational energy and connection to spirit. When whale appears, it means you're going through a time of transformation and enlightenment. Your intuition, creativity, and innate knowledge is growing rapidly during this time. Whale means you'll remain balanced as you move through these positive changes with graceful fluidity. Thought-provoking ideas will come to you, making you search deeper for answers. It's time to learn and grow and to express what you're feeling in your new knowledge. This isn't a time for remaining quiet but is for open discussion, singing, and happiness.

Whale encourages you to put your intuition to the test by actively using it. Through use, the accuracy will increase. Whale means you often say prophetic things without even realizing you're doing it. By becoming aware of whale's message of spiritual growth, you can learn to tap into your own intuitive nature and have a better understanding of what you're seeing and feeling. This will enable you to pass along intuitive messages in a more precise way.

Wildebeest (Gnu)

Element(s): Earth | Primary Color(s): Brown

When wildebeest shows up, it means you feel like you're not in control of your life. It's as if you're being herded down a path without making a conscious choice of the direction you should take. You have to go with the flow, fit in with the herd, or else be trampled. This can cause feelings of anger, disappointment, and rage at your circumstances if you let yourself fall into negative thinking. Wildebeest can help you take back control by putting you in the lead, letting you choose your own path, while the rest of the herd follows. It's all a matter of perception.

Wildebeest means you know when to retreat and when to forge ahead. You are overly aware of nearby dangers and are constantly on alert. You depend on others around you to keep you in the know and to warn you of any threats. Wildebeest means that your family bonds are strong. If you have experienced family problems lately, now is the time to resolve any conflicts. Wildebeests are known for migrating large distances. If you want to start a new relationship, or move to a new home, take a risk, make a move, and experience all that you desire in life.

Whip-poor-will (Nighthawk, Swisher)

Element(s): Air, earth | Primary Color(s): Brown

Whip-poor-will symbolizes creativity, intuition, and camouflage. Whip-poor-will is a master of hiding in plain sight. If you need to keep a secret or hide for a while, then whip-poor-will can guide you. They are very protective of their young. Whip-poor-will will even fake a broken wing in order to draw attention away from its hatchlings. Whip-poor-will also times the hatching of its eggs to the lunar cycle. This means you would benefit by learning more about the moon cycles and applying some of this knowledge to different areas of your life.

You have a hauntingly beautiful voice whether you're speaking or singing. Whip-poor-will encourages you to use your song and to listen to the sounds of the night. You do your best work at night, feel at home in the darkness, and enjoy listening to the songs of the nocturnal animals. Whip-poor-will means you're entering a period of transition, phasing out the old and bringing in the new. It's a time of growth in all areas of your life and whip-poor-will can help you easily adapt to the changes coming your way.

Wolf

Element(s): Earth, water | Primary Color(s): Black, brown, gray, red

Wolf symbolizes wildness, independence, a courageous nature, solitude, loyalty, a pack frame of mind and sense of community, a curious nature, and strong will. Social, affectionate, and always finding time for fun, wolf empowers you to embrace the calm wildness within yourself.

When wolf appears, positivity is coming your way in the form of new prospects. Make sure you trust in yourself and have a high sense of clarity and integrity so you can pursue the new opportunities when they show up.

Be sincere in your dealings with loved ones. You tend to avoid confrontations whenever possible but will fight to defend those you love. It's time to let go of that which no longer serves you, both in your personal life, work environment, and spiritually. You are very passionate, have a defined sense of social order, but can be shy with others outside of your immediate circle. If you're feeling like a lone wolf, isolated from the rest of the pack, now is the time to let go of past grievances and clear up any misunderstandings in order to regain the closeness of the group.

Wolverine

Element(s): Earth | Primary Color(s): Brown

Wolverine symbolizes power, strength, and courage. Wolverine appears when you're going to need to take a stand. It means you're willing to fight, and when you do, it's ferocious. You have high ideals and are set in your beliefs. You don't like to compromise and prefer things to happen your way. Wolverine means that you won't back down from anyone or anything. Sometimes this isn't the best idea, so wolverine warns you to pick your battles and not to be a hothead or go off the deep end because of an imagined wrong. Wolverine can go into a blood thirsty rage and warns you not to lose your temper this way because being overly aggressive can get you into trouble.

Wolverine means that you have thick skin and a high tolerance for pain. Just make sure that you don't mask your pain and hide it so deeply that it has a negative effect on you. Wolverine is adaptable and resourceful, as are you. It can give you intense focus and once you dig into something you don't let it go. You're committed and unwavering. Once committed to something or someone, you are in for the long haul.

Woodpecker

Element(s): Air | Primary Color(s): Black, red, white, yellow

Woodpecker symbolizes recognizing when opportunity is knocking. When woodpecker appears, it is a sign to figure things out on your own, to look at what has you puzzled, and to find an imaginative and distinctive way to solve the issue. It's telling you that now is the time to take action, openly communicate with others, and pay attention to details. Woodpecker is a sign of prophecy, of something you have been sensing coming to fruition.

Woodpecker means you need to rely on your own expertise, knowledge, and perspective and apply what you know to the job at hand instead of asking for someone else's opinion. Woodpecker doesn't back away until it has completed its goal, and neither do you. You can be hard-headed when you're after something. Woodpecker warns not to become obsessed but to flow within your natural rhythm. Woodpecker also shows up when you're being repetitive, stuck in the same way of doing things over and over, and need to break free from it. Woodpecker will show you different ways to accomplish the same task. It can show you how to follow a new and exciting path that is still your own.

Zebra

Element(s): Earth | Primary Color(s): Black, white

Zebra symbolizes balance, community, and individuality. When zebra appears, it means you're looking at a situation as all or nothing when it's not that way. Zebra shows you that situations are not always categorized in absolutes. Zebra urges you to see the gray areas between the lines, the part where the black and white blends together. Sometimes it is in this gray area where the most important discoveries are made.

Zebra can help you find balance between your daily life and your spirituality. Sometimes you may feel your intuitive nature is making you stand out in the crowd when really all you want to do is blend in. Zebra can protect you from any perceived danger you feel because you're exposing a private part of yourself to others. You're very clairvoyant and may feel drawn to help people by using your abilities but are afraid of what the naysayers will say. Zebra urges you to follow your path and know that you are using your abilities in a positive, helpful way and you will influence and help many people. It may be hard stepping away from the herd but when you do, you'll run wild and free.

Visualization with a Specific Animal

For this visualization exercise, select the animal that you want to connect with. Let your mind drift to the environment where the animal lives. Visualize the animal going about its daily activities. Make note of the things you see, the actions of the animal, and whether or not you see other animals in the area. As you observe the animal in its natural habitat, you suddenly become aware that it has noticed you. Let your breathing slow down, watch the animal without looking it directly in the eye. What is it doing? Is it ignoring you or coming toward you? You see it start to move closer to you in a roundabout way, slowly getting closer and closer until it can smell you. You sit quietly, letting the animal connect to your essence as you wait. Then you feel a tingling sensation all around you. It's like the air has become alive with electricity crackling through the air. The animal looks directly in your eyes, so you meet its gaze. Images flash across your mind's eye, a sharing of knowledge, of emotions, of the Divine. Just as quickly as it started it's over. The animal nudges against you and then continues on its way.

Chapter Four

DOMESTICATED ANIMALS

Angelfish

Element(s): Water | Primary Color(s): Black, blue, orange,
red, silver, white, yellow, multicolored

Angelfish symbolizes living up to your fullest potential, connection to the angelic realms, and transformation. When angelfish appears, it means you are embarking on an adventure of spiritual growth. Angelfish means you will experience new intuitive abilities and the expansion of abilities you already use. If you are a lucid dreamer, you may discover that now your dreams are prophetic. If you're clairvoyant, you may also develop clairaudience.

Angelfish offers you protection from negativity while lighting your path with purity. Angelfish means others may seek your guidance about spirituality or understanding their own gifts. You feel comfortable in your ability to guide and direct others. Angelfish is connected to emotions, so your empathic abilities will start to become clearer. In decision-making, angelfish can show you areas that need further investigation before you make a final decision. It allows you to see clearly in the darkest water. Angelfish offers assurance that whatever path you choose, it will be the right one for you at this time.

Camel

Element(s): Earth | Primary Color(s): Brown

Camel symbolizes reserving your energy, taking a journey, and being of service to others. Camel means being able to survive in any type of harsh conditions because you are resourceful and resilient. When camel appears, it means to look within yourself for empowerment and clarity instead of seeking it from other people. You have everything you need to survive. Now is the time for you to be self-reliant and stand on your own. You are your own inspiration, cheerleader, and teacher. You carry your own burdens instead of sharing them with others.

Camel means not to waste your energy on things that aren't completely necessary to your survival. Camel stores fat in its humps to use when it is without food or water. Camel means you're giving away too much of your time and energy to others instead of keeping it in reserve or you're burning it up way too fast. Now is the time to step back and let others rely on themselves and to slow down your fast pace. Build up your reserves. You may need them sooner than you think. Camel assists when you need to be of service to others.

Canary

Element(s): Air | Primary Color(s): Green, red, yellow

Canary symbolizes the power of song, speech, and creative expression. Canary means sound is important to you and a key connection to the spiritual realm. People enjoy hearing what you have to say because your sound energy touches them on a deep level and brings light to their lives. Canary means to convey more joy and happiness in your life by recognizing the power of your own voice. You speak up for yourself and sing your own song instead of replicating the songs of others, which makes you a unique personality. You are filled with light and joy and it's time to share your song with the world.

Canary means you may help someone on their spiritual journey or teach them how to develop their intuitive abilities. Creative expression with sound is your strength. You may excel in sound healing and sound therapy to raise your consciousness and connect to spirit. Words are powerful, precise, and, if used as a weapon, can cut as deep as a knife. It is your responsibility, as a light being, to ensure your words are spoken clearly with precision to lift others up, encourage, and enlighten.

Carp

Element(s): Water | Primary Color(s): Brown, silver, yellow

Carp symbolizes travel, reproduction, and growth. Carp means you are in a time of growth and whatever you pursue at this time will expand to massive proportions. Expect to travel as you pursue your endeavors. When carp appears, it means you need to make sure you're not muddying the waters, stirring up trouble, or being irritating to those around you. While your plans are taking off and you're moving into new territory, try to build friendships instead of making those who are already established feel threatened.

Carp is considered the boniest creature on earth. It has a whopping 4,386 bones. This means your internal support system is strong, multilayered, and you often rely on your own intricate foundation instead of asking others for help. This can be off-putting to others when you're establishing yourself in a new venture, so make sure you handle yourself with finesse. Carp means you're always growing, you adapt well to any conditions you find yourself in, and, while you may be messy and unorganized at times, you do whatever you have to do to succeed. Hard work and getting dirty doesn't bother you one little bit.

Visualization with Cat

Imagine... You've been out of town for a few days and when you return to your house there is a white cat sitting by your front door. It's well groomed but doesn't have a collar and looks on the thin side. You don't have pets, so you try to shoo it away. That doesn't work because it gets up and starts rubbing around your legs, purring very loudly with happiness. You push it away as you enter the house, but before you can close the door it streaks inside. You find it in the kitchen, sitting in front of the sink looking up at the cabinets. You make it some food and watch it eat. You post fliers everywhere looking for the owner. No one ever shows, so you name it and keep it as your guardian.

Cat

*Element(s): Earth | Primary Color(s): Black, brown, gray,
orange, white, various mixed colors and patterns*

Cat symbolizes harmony, timing, and exploration of the unknown. When cat appears, it means you need to be patient, stay quiet, and just observe what is happening around you. Timing is important to cat. It will wait until just the right time to attack its prey or make a move. This means to wait before taking action to ensure you're in the best possible position to obtain your goal.

You're an excellent communicator who is independent and likes time alone but who is also comfortable being part of a group. You enjoy being outside in the sun but usually work best at night. Cat means you need to be more flexible and harmonious in your relationships with others. Sometimes you can be too unpredictable, only heeding your own instincts without regard to others. While you'll always land on your feet, others around you may not, and will need your assistance to get back on track. Cat assists when you need to find what is hidden in the dark. Cats are mystical creatures that can see in the dark and will enlighten you on the path of self-discovery.

Cattle (Cow)

Element(s): Earth | Primary Color(s): Black, brown, red, white, multiple patterns

When cow appears, it means you need to take it slow and easy and enjoy life. You often tend to do too many things at one time, while putting the needs of others before yourself. Like cow, you can function without much sleep and still feel rested (cows only sleep about four hours a day). Cow has excellent panoramic vision and can see almost 360 degrees. This means you need to look at everything around you, pay attention to details, and evaluate what is happening before taking action.

Cow means you are steadfast and stand your ground even if a storm is brewing around you. Cow has a sixth sense about danger and knows where the best grazing lands are. Cow can lead you to understand your own innate intuitive abilities and lead you out of dangerous situations to a better place. Assists when you need to make sure you're taking care of your basic needs in order to help others. Cow can teach you how to have stability in your life without being inflexible. It can show you how to move forward without wasting your energy while teaching others the importance of patience and persistence.

Chameleon

Element(s): Air, earth | Primary Color(s): Many colors combined in many different patterns

Chameleon symbolizes change, blending in, and alertness. When chameleon appears, it means that there are things going on that you may not be aware of, so pay close attention and look around to discover what is lurking nearby. Chameleon is not deaf, but it doesn't hear very well. What it lacks in hearing it makes up for in eyesight. This means to rely on what you're seeing as truth more than what you hear.

Chameleon can move slowly, creeping up unnoticed, and then strike out with its tongue at lightning speed to catch its prey. You need to move slowly and when the moment is right, strike quickly to achieve your goals. This is a time of change. You prefer being alone but may find yourself involved with a group. You'll intuitively know if you should blend in with the crowd or stand out and make your presence known. Chameleon warns against compromising your own beliefs or morals or letting other people's opinions influence you. You're steadfast and sensitive and have precise timing. You're able to see a person's real intention. It's important for you to stay true to your own colors.

Chicken

Element(s): Earth | Primary Color(s): Black, brown, red, white

When chicken appears, it means to look out for someone who may take advantage of your generous nature. Since you see the good in people, are very nurturing to others, and often put them first, especially family, you often don't see or even think about any type of manipulative or negative behavior until you're looking at a situation in hindsight. Chicken means to use your imagination and bring your creativity to life in whatever form you prefer.

Chicken is very intuitive, especially empathic, and is closely connected to the earth. When earth energy accumulates within chicken, it can become nervous, ill-tempered, and have unpredictable behavior. This means to find some way to balance your own energy and find an outlet for it so that it doesn't build up and send you into an explosion of squawking. Chicken is a sign of new birth. While this can be a physical birth of a child, it is more often indicative of the birth of a new business, partnership, or other venture. Chicken assists when you need to improve your memory. It can remember more than a hundred different faces of people or other animals.

Chinchilla

Element(s): Earth | Primary Color(s): Gray, white

When chinchilla appears, it means to keep your secrets close, remain silent, and to give deep thought to the situations in your life. You're very curious, and in watching you will discover many secrets that others hold close but reveal when they think no one is looking. Chinchilla is mysterious, intuitive, and reflects innocence yet maintains self-control. This means you should retain your own mystery by not revealing all of your secrets. You are able to see someone's inner essence and know if they are deserving of your trust. Chinchilla urges you to embrace your intuitive Divine nature to enhance your connection to ancient and universal knowledge so you will continually experience growth in your lifetime.

Chinchilla takes dust baths to clean itself because its fur is so dense it has a hard time drying if it gets wet. This means you have to get dirty to find clarity. Take time to work outside. Chinchilla likes to sit in high places and look down at the world. This means to connect to your higher self in order to find ways you can grow on your spiritual path.

Cockatiel (Cockatoo, Parakeet)

Element(s): Air | Primary Color(s): Gray, pink, white, yellow

When cockatiel appears, it means you work well with others and are a clear communicator with a high level of intelligence. Cockatiel urges you to speak your feelings and thoughts instead of keeping them locked up inside. Cockatiel is a colorful bird, which means you often have a vibrant personality and enjoy bright, shiny things.

Cockatiel likes to stay busy. It can get bored easily, so it's important to always have toys, perches, and swings so it'll have something to do. You can also become bored or distracted if you don't have things to keep your mind occupied. Flying is an important part of cockatiel's life. It needs time outside of its cage to fly around the house if you haven't clipped its wings. For you, this means you need to soar. Go to the park and swing, go hang gliding, or climb a tree to get a feeling of height and the wind moving around you. Cockatiel is known for its exotic looks—its beautiful crest, sleek feathers, and colorful face. If cockatiel appears, it means to take more time with your appearance. Cockatiel warns against being too rash and gruff with your words.

Dog

*Element(s): Earth | Primary Color(s): Black, brown,
white, yellow*

Dog symbolizes loyalty, protection, and service. When dog appears, the first thing to do is consider the breed of dog and the unique characteristics of that breed. If it's a Chihuahua, it means your bark is louder than your bite; if it's a German shepherd, then you may need to be extra vigilant about protection. Dog means you have to remain faithful to yourself and what you want to accomplish in life, regardless of the distractions around you. When dog appears, it is a sign you should remain strong in your intention and have faith that everything will work out as it should. If you've been too hard or critical of yourself and others or are in attack mode, dog can help you see the positive over the negative and find your way back to your true loving and noble nature.

Dog sees the good in everything and encourages you to do the same. Dog warns that you should always sniff out the people around you and the situations you're in to find the truth. If something smells off, even if you can't figure out what it is, listen to dog and pay close attention to discover what is hidden.

Donkey

Element(s): Earth | Primary Color(s): Brown, gray, white

When donkey appears, it is a sign of spiritual growth. It's time to embrace and grow your intuition, empathic abilities, and connection to the Divine. Donkey means you may be taking on too much in an effort to help others and sometimes you need to let them stand on their own two feet. Donkey warns to be alert in case someone is trying to take advantage of your helpful nature.

You are analytical and tend to evaluate situations before taking action. Like donkey, if you decide a situation is dangerous or could have complications that will directly affect you, no one will change your mind regardless of how much they try to convince you otherwise. This isn't stubbornness but a keen sense of self-preservation through both analytical skill and intuitive insight. Donkey has a solid, stable character, is gentle and kind, but can be fiercely protective. You share these qualities with donkey. People often don't expect to see aggressive or protective behavior from you because you're so willing to help other people and are gentle and kind. Donkey assists when you need to say no.

Duck

Element(s): Air, earth, water | Primary Color(s): Mixture of many different colors and patterns

When duck appears, it means you need to find a better way to handle your stress levels. When you're too uptight, on edge, and quick to anger, stress is usually the culprit. Duck can show you how to balance between water, earth, and air so you release the agitation, let go of worry, and find balance. You can connect to these three elements and duck energy to quickly get settled if you start feeling off-kilter. Duck is comfortable in all kinds of situations and can lend you its easygoing nature to help you feel at ease too.

Ducks flock together, which means you know many people. That being said, you only have a few trusted friends who are close to you. If you find you're being too inflexible in any part of your life, duck can show you how to loosen up and be more flexible by looking at many different ways of doing things instead of sticking to your preferred methods. Duck can help you be emotionally strong, and when your emotions are high to see through them to find balance. Duck encourages you to live in the moment instead of dwelling on the past or worrying about the future.

Ferret

Element(s): Earth | Primary Color(s): Black, brown, gray, white

Ferret symbolizes the fierce nature of a hunter and the wisdom of the universe. While ferret is quick to defend itself with a strong bite, it can also serve as your messenger for and connection to universal knowledge. When ferret appears, it means to look for hidden meanings. This is a time for emotional and spiritual growth, to trust your instincts, and to delve into new and unexplored territory. Working through emotions can be difficult, but ferret gives you the intuitive insight to get to the root of problems as you lift layer upon layer of emotions away to get to the cause. You're highly motivated to make changes in your life at this time and ferret will push, pull, and snap at your heels to get you there, acting as your guardian along the way.

Ferret also means you're coming into a time of financial growth. Ferret encourages you to trust your vision and sense of smell. When something looks and smells good, then go for it, but if it appears that all is not as it seems or smells off to you, then look closer for hidden agendas and steer clear. Ferret reminds you to remember to have a good sense of humor.

❧

Elemental Meanings

Some animals have a primary element where they spend the majority of their time and others spend their time equally in two or more elements, so you'd want to consider each of the elements. Think of where your energy animal spends most of its time. For example, horses spend the majority of their time on land, but they also like to swim. Since the time spent swimming and being on land isn't equal, the horse's element would be earth. Ducks, on the other hand, spend their time equally on land, in the water, and in the air, so they would share all three. Animals that live in the trees would have the element of air, if they spend more time in the trees than on the ground. The better you understand the nature of your energy animal and its environment, the better your frequency connection with it will be.

Air	Adapts well to changes, carries away troubles, communication
Earth	The ability to find and use resources, absorbs excesses of the other elements, adventure
Fire	Astounding depth of emotions, attracts others, cleansing
Water	Active imagination, cleansing, creativity

Gerbil

Element(s): Earth | Primary Color(s): Black, brown, gold, gray, silver, white, multicolored

When gerbil appears, it means to connect to the things that make you feel the most comfortable and secure. You may feel drawn to being alone and spending time creating new projects, particularly crafts with intricate details. You pay attention to the small things in life that others may not notice. Gerbil is social but has no fear of exploring on its own. If you've become too much of a homebody, now is the time to get out of the house and do something.

Gerbil can show you how to dig in and create something unique and intriguing. You may discover that others aren't as interested in your work as you believe they should be, or they don't take what you're attempting seriously, especially when it comes to artistry. Gerbil encourages you to continue on your path. Being artistic is part of you, and you excel at it. Be proud of your creations, pursue your dreams, and don't let anyone hold you back. Believe in yourself and you can do anything. Experiencing new things, even at the risk of feeling uncomfortable, will help you grow as a person.

Goat

Element(s): Earth | Primary Color(s): Black, brown, gray, red,
white, mixture of colors and patterns

When goat appears, it means that now is the time to take one step at a time, being cautious and practical. Like goat, you are determined and don't let obstacles stand in your way. There are times when you can move forward very quickly, jumping to new heights and being a bit reckless in your pursuits. Now is not one of those times. Instead, remain determined and fearless and access your inner strength to make calculated choices on your path. While you are open to listening to the advice of others, if the advice doesn't intuitively seem correct for the situation, then look to your higher self for alternative solutions.

Goat means you will make great achievements because you don't give up when you set your mind toward a goal. Goat warns against overindulgent behavior, relying on others too much, or giving up too soon. The path to success can be a long one, but you're up for the journey. Goat helps when you need to open yourself and make a conscious effort to examine your emotions.

Goldfish (Koi)

Element(s): Water | Primary Color(s): Gold, orange

Goldfish symbolizes transformation, growth, good fortune, and adaptability. Goldfish has long been a symbol of good luck in many cultures. It is connected to the spiritual realm, which means that growth and positive transformation is on your horizon. When goldfish appears, it means you're entering a time of luck and change. Everything you attempt will turn to gold, be positive, and bring prosperity your way. There are changes coming to you at this time but you will easily flow and adapt to them as they occur.

Goldfish means to open your mind to new possibilities and opportunities. You are optimistic, interact well with others, and have a bright personality. These qualities draw influential people to you who have ideas that will cause you to start a new business or come up with a concept that will be highly marketable and prosperous. This is also time to keep quiet about any ideas, inventions, or projects. Goldfish will help you remain silent so you have time to create and manifest to bring them to fruition. Goldfish means to look for the enjoyment and fun in situations instead of taking yourself too seriously.

Goose

Element(s): Earth, water | Primary Color(s): Black, brown,
gray, white

Goose symbolizes family, love, and affection. Now is the time to surround yourself with those you love. Goose also represents fertility, so you, or someone close to you, may find out a new baby is on the way. When goose appears, it means to analyze whether you should lead or follow. Goose is exceptionally good in both roles, as are you, and knows when each is appropriate. Goose is an excellent communicator with its loud, distinctive honk.

Goose warns against getting so involved in the lives of others that you forget your own purpose and pursuits. While others may have good intentions by offering direction, ultimately you choose your own path, which leads to spiritual growth and enlightenment. Goose reminds you to remember your true self and life purpose. It assists when you need to make the best of a situation. Goose is wise, offers protection, and will lash out if it feels threatened. These qualities will help you feel comfortable if you're unsure about a situation you're involved in. It can help you find balance and guide you to areas where your energy is best utilized.

Guinea Fowl

Element(s): Earth | Primary Color(s): Black, blue, gray, white

When guinea fowl appears, it means working in groups. It is a very social bird that interacts in small groups. Guinea fowl means to connect to your spiritual self, to listen to your intuition, and to voice your knowledge with confidence and authority. Guinea fowl typically mates for life, which means love and family are important to you. Its mating display is to chase each other and then circle around one another flapping their wings. It is believed that universal power and spiritual strength move from the Divine to earth through circles and spirals. This means for you to spend time connecting to your own spirituality and determining what you believe to be your own universal truths.

The helmeted guinea fowl has what looks like a spur protruding from the top of its head like a helmet. Don't succumb to peer pressure and not wear protective head gear whether you're riding a horse, motorcycle, skateboard, or bicycle. It's better to be safe now, than to be sorry later. Guinea fowl assists when you need to defend yourself or run from a negative situation. It can help keep pesky situations and people at bay.

Guinea Pig (Hamster)

Element(s): Earth | Primary Color(s): Black, brown, gray,
red, white, multicolored

Guinea pig symbolizes spiritual growth, connecting with like-minded people, and welcoming new ideas. When guinea pig appears, it means to watch your diet. It can't produce vitamin C and needs a supplement to make sure it's getting the required amount. Guinea pig can't sweat, so it prefers cooler, shady environments but not too cold, as it can also get chilled. This means you need to watch your water intake and make sure you're not getting over-heated during activities.

Guinea pigs are avid groomers. This means you should take extra care of your appearance and practice good hygiene. They are also born with all of their fur, with their eyes open, and able to eat solid food, however they can't see what's directly in front of them, which means they can't see what they're eating and is a warning not to overeat. You also have everything you need within you. By connecting to your spiritual self, you will be able to excel in all that you set out to achieve. Guinea pig warns to look at situations from all angles because sometimes you don't see what's right in front of you.

Guppy

Element(s): Water | Primary Color(s): Many different colors

When guppy appears, it means you can easily adapt to any situation you find yourself in. If you're unsure how to handle yourself, guppy suggests hiding out of sight to watch what's going on and then make decisions on how to move forward. When a pregnant guppy and fry are tired, they retreat to the safety of the plants in its tank to hide away and rest, all the while keeping an eye on its environment. If their environment becomes overcrowded, guppy will eat its fry. This means you too may need a separation from family or those closest to you in order to rest or to make important decisions and to flourish.

Guppy has been deliberately set free in a multitude of countries in order to fight the spread of malaria because they eat mosquito larvae. This means you are able to do many good deeds, but you have to let yourself be free to do them. So let go of any negative feelings or doubt you may have about yourself, go out into the world and make an impression, leave your mark, make the world a better place. Guppy assists when you need to increase your financial portfolio or store supplies for a rainy day.

Hedgehog

Element(s): Earth | Primary Color(s): Black, brown, gray, white

When hedgehog appears, it means other people don't understand you or are asking too much of you. You're a very gifted person, you have a big heart and help out whenever you're needed, but people may think you're a little quirky because they don't get your sense of humor, your personality, or the path you've chosen to take.

You're closely connected to the energy of the earth and are at one with your intuition and spirituality. You often manifest what you need in your life and are open to receive what is coming to you. You have the ability to teach others how to connect to their own spirituality and understand their own unique gifts. You have the gift of sight, which is indicated by hedgehog's ability to see better in the dark than in daylight. You also tend to have visions and prophetic dreams. Hedgehog has poor eyesight and relies on its senses of smell and hearing. This means you too must use all of your senses and abilities in life. Things will flow more smoothly and with much more clarity if you remain connected to your core essence.

VISUALIZATION WITH HORSE

Imagine ... You're in the barn. There's something unique about the mixture of smells—the horses, shavings, and hay. You walk over to your horse's stall and greet your mare, rubbing her nose through the rails. You go inside and hug her around her neck. You breathe deeply, inhaling her scent, feeling your heart connect with hers as she lowers her head on your back and pulls you closer in a warm hug. You smile against her neck, feeling content and happy. You think about the beautiful being that she is; she takes your breath away with her movement, but this ... this is what it's all about ... the deep, unbreakable bond between kindred spirits.

Horse

Element(s): Earth | Primary Color(s): Black, brown, gray, red,
white, many other colors and patterns

Horse symbolizes loyalty, friendship, trust, and working together. Horse appears when you are feeling confined, restless, and on edge. It means you need to run free, to work out the restlessness through exercise, and to feel the wind in your face. This will bring you back in balance, calm you, and help you work out solutions to any problems you are facing. Independence and freedom are important to you but you are also willing, giving, and able to bond closely to those who treat you with love and respect.

Horse means you're about to embark on a new journey. You may be traveling or the journey may be a spiritual one where you expand your consciousness of mind, body, and spirit. You have unbelievable stamina and keep going until the job is done, even if you're tired. You never give up on those you love or on your pursuit of your dreams. Horse means that sometimes you need to take a break from the weight you carry, to get back in touch with your own inner needs. Horse warns to take things in stride instead of letting fear cause you to be spooked or rebellious.

Iguana

Element(s): Air, earth, water | Primary Color(s): Blue, green, red, turquoise, white

Iguana symbolizes acceptance, awareness, and self-confidence. When iguana appears, it means to be more observant of your surroundings and to open to your senses by using your third eye. Give everything you see your full attention and consideration. You will find that the world is awe-inspiring. Iguana can show you your life's purpose and true nature.

Iguana encourages you to let go of worries. Don't let life pass you by because you're obsessing over things. Iguana means to get outside and spend time basking in the sunlight. Feel the sun's warmth on your face and let it fill you, energize you, bring you closer to your spiritual self. Connect to your higher self, find your own inner light, and move upward in regard to your own spirituality. You're embarking on a path of tremendous spiritual growth. Iguana can show you how to slow down, return to center, appreciate your life to the fullest, and simply be within the stillness of the moment. Iguana can help you let go of the things holding you in stressful patterns so you can better appreciate your life.

Llama (Alpaca)

Element(s): Earth | Primary Color(s): Black, brown, gray, white, variety of patterns

When llama appears, it means you're carrying too much responsibility on your own shoulders. Llama is a very social animal that solves disputes by spitting at one another. If you don't have time for social events or relaxing with family and friends due to your busy schedule, llama urges you to make changes before you get to the point where you can no longer move because the weight is so heavy. Don't turn into a control freak; instead, let go of some of the control to free up your burden. Llama means you have to take care of yourself before you can take care of others.

Llama is also connected to the spiritual realm, especially clairaudience. This means you often hear messages from the spiritual and angelic realms. When llama appears it means you can see your destination on the horizon. Llama means to take your time, move slowly but steadily, keep your balance, and make sure you know where your feet are at all times. Awareness and balance are keys to your success. Llama is also a sign of being too stubborn. Are you?

Lory (Rainbow)

Element(s): Air | Primary Color(s): Black, blue, green, orange, red, yellow

When lory appears, it means to go after what you want instead of waiting for it to come to you. Lory is a very colorful bird. Lory urges you to find the vibrancy and joyful colors in your life. Lory can show you all of the possible outcomes to enable easier decision-making. Lory means to think things through. It is a highly intelligent bird that can figure things out, learn tricks, talk, and easily escapes its cage unless it's locked. Lory urges you to use your own intelligence. You'll always be able to escape an uncomfortable or stressful situation if you have lory as a guide.

Lory means to respect your own individuality. Embrace all of your unique quirks, your faults, and your gifts. Lory assists when you need to better understand and respect someone's point of view. When you look at what someone is saying from both sides of the spectrum, it will give you a clearer understanding of why they feel the way they do about a subject. Lory can help you understand every viewpoint in complex situations so you can make clear and unbiased decisions while forming your own opinion.

Mule

Element(s): Earth | Primary Color(s): Black, brown, red, white

Mule symbolizes independence, intelligence, and wisdom. When mule appears, it means to trust in your own strengths, rely on your own wit and intelligence, and make sure you're capable of handling the things you take on. Mule means you're a strong person with strength of character who prefers working alone. Mule reminds you that sometimes a very heavy load needs to be carried by more than one and it's okay to ask for help.

Mule gets its intelligence from the donkey and its athleticism from the horse. For you, this means that while you can do the work asked of you, if you feel unsafe or if it is illogical then you have no problem refusing. When mule appears, it means to check yourself to see if you're being overly cautious simply because you don't want to be bothered to do the task at hand. Mule is also known for its long ears, so make sure you're really listening to and understanding what others are saying to you. Use your keen sense of hearing to listen for insinuated meanings, things that are there in tone and pitch but are not voiced in words.

Pig

Element(s): Earth, water | Primary Color(s): Black, red, white

When pig appears, it means financial changes are coming soon. Pig is associated with money, luck, and the improvement of finances. This means you need to be aware that your personal financial picture is about to change and make sure it changes for the better. Pig is also associated with the law of attraction, which is when you manifest your desires through intuition, creative visualization, and positive thoughts. So, if you've been considering investments but are unsure about them, then your doubt is your intuition saying to wait.

The changes pig brings can be either positive or negative, but when you're aware, you can avoid the negative most of the time. This also means that if you think of what you want in the wrong way, you can also inadvertently bring negativity to you. So make sure your manifestation is always positive and precise. Pig means focus, determination, and change. When pig is focused on something, it is utterly focused and you'd be hard-pressed to lure it away from what has its attention (like food). Pig and its determined nature ensures success. It assists when you need to find balance.

Pigeon

Element(s): Air | Primary Color(s): Gray, white

When pigeon appears, it means to look upward to find your success. Pigeon can fly nearly straight up, which is a sign to look to your own spirituality in order to connect to the Divine. Pigeon means to access your inner intuition and universal flow to find your way safely home again. If you don't feel content or secure in your home, it's time to evaluate where you're living. Is it time to move or make other changes that will make you feel safe?

Pigeon means to look at your youth for answers, especially if you've been feeling restless and on edge, as if you're missing something in your life. It's not always easy to go home again but if you can, return to your roots in order to strengthen your foundation or explore your heritage. Pigeon urges you to be determined in your spiritual quest or in finding answers to any questions you have. Pigeon will not leave an area as long as it can find food. You can shoo it away, other birds can try to chase it away, but until it is ready to leave, pigeon will stay put. This is a great lesson in understanding how to stay the course to overcome obstacles in your path.

Praying Mantis

Element(s): Earth | Primary Color(s): Brown, green

Praying mantis symbolizes spirituality, mindfulness, and inner wisdom. When praying mantis appears, it means to embrace your creativity. Allow the flow of universal energy to bring concepts to you. When the right one comes along, it will feel right and you'll be able to give it power and positivity so it can grow into a productive project.

Praying mantis also means to take time to just be. Commune with nature, soak in a hot bath, or listen to soothing music. When you push aside the noise of life and listen to your inner voice, that's when you'll get the best ideas and make the best discoveries about your own spirituality. Praying mantis means you need a little peace and quiet, so when you return to the hectic pace of life you will have quick reflexes and it will be easier to follow your instincts. Praying mantis has excellent eyesight and can see something move up to sixty feet away and can turn its head 180 degrees. This means you need to not only pay attention to what's happening close to you but look in the near distance as well.

Rabbit

Element(s): Earth | Primary Color(s): Black, brown, gray, white

When rabbit appears, it means you need to pay attention to what's happening around you so you can react quickly to the abundance of opportunities coming your way. Rabbit has 360-degree panoramic vision, which lets it see everything except one spot directly in front of its nose. This means not to miss something right in front of you.

Rabbit is affectionate and has a gentle nature. If you've been distant or belligerent in your relationships because of past hurts, rabbit can show you how to regain the gentleness within your soul. Rabbit means you are focusing too much on the things you fear or that worry you. Let go of the fear because it is holding you back. Once you do, you'll find you're able to move forward in leaps and bounds. Rabbit encourages you to have fun in life. When feeling happy and playful, rabbit will twist its body and flick its feet while jumping high into the air. Its coordination and clever intellect helps them get out of tight spots or difficult situations. Rabbit urges you to stay ready to act, react, and move when necessary to ensure your success.

Sheep

Element(s): Earth | Primary Color(s): Black, brown, gray, red, silver, white

Sheep symbolizes innocence and vulnerability. When sheep appears, it means you will encounter a situation where you will have to obey the rules of tradition. You have a strong desire to fit into your groups and to have other people like you, so you conform to what is happening around you. Sheep warns against trying too hard to please someone else because you can lose your individuality.

If sheep appears, you are ready to commit to developing your intuition, understanding your spirituality, and taking care of your higher self. This will be a time of great self-discovery, a time of learning and exploring ideas that may seem foreign to you at first but are a touchstone to your soul. Seek guidance from those who have walked the path, but don't become part of the crowd, instead ask questions for yourself, take what feels right for your own spiritual growth, and leave the rest to consider again later. Sheep assists when you need to recapture the happiness and innocence of your childhood. Sheep can show you how to get those feelings back again in order to look at life through different eyes.

Siamese Fighting Fish (Betta Fish)

Element(s): Water | Primary Color(s): Black, blue, brown,
gold, green, indigo, orange, pink, purple, red, silver,
turquoise, white, yellow

When betta fish appears, it means you're undergoing a spiritual awakening and will have more contact with the spiritual realms. Now is the time to let go of any aggressive feelings you may have, to understand why you're having them, and to uncover the root cause of those feelings. Learn as much as you can through books and articles about spirituality, intuition, and any other similar topic to which you feel a connection. Expect to experience a greater connection with the spiritual realm, including guides, angels, and master teachers. You may have more prophetic dreams, visions, or be able to better understand any intuitive impressions you receive.

Betta fish means you easily adapt to changes in your life, are independent, and are filled with positive potential. Once you tap into your inner truth, you will go far and achieve much success. Betta fish can help you spend time alone to analyze and understand your own ego and the root cause of any confrontational or negative feelings.

Silkworm (Silk Moth)

Element(s): Air, earth | Primary Color(s): White

When silkworm appears, it means you're being healed from the inside out. You may not even be aware of the changes happening within you, but you are growing and developing, transforming into a beautiful being filled with intuition, faith, and the uncanny ability to find the light in the darkest of nights. When you realize the changes you've made, it will come as a surprise but you will feel as if you're one with the secret knowledge of the universe.

Silkworm means you will attract like-minded individuals to your calm serenity. You may begin to experience deeper intuitive impressions, powerful dreams, and strong psychic abilities. Silkworm reminds you that difficult situations always pass in time and it is up to you to see the beauty in the outcome. Silkworm can lay three to four hundred eggs at a time. This indicates that anything you attempt right now will be fertile and successful. Silkworm warns against hiding from your own emotions. Silkworm reminds you to do for yourself instead of letting others take care of your needs. It assists when you need to be more creative.

Society Finch

Element(s): Air | Primary Color(s): Black, brown,
gray, red, white

When society finch appears, it means there will be more opportunities for livelihood, mingling, and social events. Society finch is a songbird, which means to sing your own unique song while enjoying the changes and activity around you. Society finch amplifies the positives in your life, allowing you to leave any negative situations in the past. Society finch changes your outlook to one of positivity, happiness, and joy.

Life is a journey and society finch implores you to live it with passion and vitality. Society finch means not to waste time on negative situations or people. It can help you find balance in situations and in dealing with people who are always procrastinating or complaining. Your joyful attitude can rub off on them, allowing them to change their point of view. Lift your wings and fly with enthusiasm. If you're in a career where you have to promote your work, make public speaking appearances, or attend social events, society finch can give you the presence and courage to put yourself out there for all to see. You encourage interaction from others and enjoy vibrant discussions.

Squirrel Monkey

Element(s): Air, earth | Primary Color(s): Black, brown, gray, green (olive), red, yellow

When squirrel monkey appears, it means to connect to your senses in a deeper, more intuitive way. Instead of just looking, see with your clairvoyance. Instead of just hearing, listen with clairaudience.

Squirrel monkey lives between earth and sky in the middle part of the tops of trees. Because of its small size, it rarely goes to the treetops or down to earth. This means you also have the ability to travel between worlds and are a medium who can connect with those who have passed to the other side. Squirrel monkey reminds you to keep balance between these realms. It's easy to get drawn into communication with the other side so much so that you ignore the human existence you're living in.

Squirrel monkey urges you to look at all situations from multiple points of view before making decisions about the situation. Change your perspective to get a clearer vision of what's happening around you. If you're unsure where you're headed in your life, if you feel lost or stuck in the past, squirrel monkey can show you how to move forward and the best future route to take.

Sugar Glider

Element(s): Air, earth | Primary Color(s): Brown, white

When sugar glider appears, it means to look at how you're interacting with people. A sugar glider male marks the members of its group with his scent. If any others try to become part of the group, he will violently chase them away. Sometimes you will experience personal and spiritual growth by meeting and interacting with new people. Sugar glider assists when you want to bond with others in more meaningful ways. If your relationships are lacking feelings of closeness, sugar glider can show you how to deepen your interactions to develop the intimacy you desire. Sugar glider can teach you how to trust others and, most importantly, how to trust yourself.

Sugar glider sleeps all day and is up at night. It does this to protect itself from predators. You may also do your best work at night, so consider nighttime careers. The sugar glider is a marsupial gliding opossum that keeps its young in its pouch. This means you have all you need within you. When you take note of the little things and apply them to your ideas, you will come up with phenomenal inventions or new ways of doing things. You feel energized by the creative process.

Tortoise

Element(s): Earth, water | Primary Color(s): Black, brown, yellow

When tortoise appears, it means to slow down. If you've been going at a fast pace for a while, now is the time to stop and really look at what is happening around you. Pay attention to both the big events and the small details. When you're constantly on the go, you often overlook things you really should see and be aware of. Tortoise means to use your resources wisely, not wastefully and to make the most of the things you have.

Tortoise is patient, persistent, and easygoing. It doesn't have drama in its life and can help you eliminate the things that make you feel overwhelmed, stressed, or that cause you worry. On the other hand, if you've been moving in slow motion, are unmotivated, or feel you don't have purpose, tortoise can help you move a little faster, pick up the pace a bit, set goals, and move forward at a steady rate to accomplish them. Tortoise assists when you need lasting progress. When you're pursuing a long-term goal, tortoise can help you find the best path to take to reach it. By taking small, steady steps and building on a solid foundation, you can pace yourself to accomplish your task.

Turkey

*Element(s): Earth | Primary Color(s): Black, brown, white,
and red and blue on its neck*

Turkey symbolizes sacrifice, abundance, and prosperity. When turkey appears, it means you're about to reap rewards of some kind. Turkey isn't only about receiving monetary wealth for the good things you do but to receive both intellectual and spiritual rewards.

Turkey means you give from the heart and go out of your way to help others. Turkey is connected to the spiritual realm and the knowledge that all life is connected and sacred. You give and work with others not out of a sense of what you'll receive in return but because you feel it is the right thing for you to do on your spiritual path. Turkey also means to honor yourself and the gifts you receive from others, whether it is emotional support or assistance with your own spiritual awakening. Spiritually, turkey means you have risen above indulging in doing things for yourself and have moved into a higher frequency where you acknowledge and strive toward universal oneness. At this level, turkey gives you feelings of contentment and satisfaction as you live in harmony with all that is.

Yak

*Element(s): Earth | Primary Color(s): Black, brown, gray,
red, white*

When yak appears, it means to get in touch with your
spiritual essence and your higher self, and to understand
and connect with your life purpose. Yak is closely tied to
ancient wisdom and universal knowledge. Yak urges you
to familiarize yourself with the customs of your family
and to connect with your personal heritage. It means you
never give up, you see things in black and white, and you
know there is always a means to an end. Yak reminds you
to live in the moment. It doesn't rush and urges you to
take your time.

Yak is a social animal that lives in groups. It relies on
the herd for its survival. This means while you like to do
things your own way, sometimes you need the closeness
of family or friends to see you through difficult times. Yak
eats grass and will not eat grain like most bovine animals.
Now is a good time to pay attention to your diet. If you
have a layer of fat like yak and you want to lose weight,
stay away from the grains and graze on fresh greens for
sustenance. Yak assists when you need to gain control
over your emotions.

VISUALIZATION IN A NATURAL SETTING

Taking the time to commune with nature is a great way to connect to energy animals. For this exercise, find a place outside where you'll be uninterrupted and where you'd expect to encounter animals. Take a seat on the ground, maybe even lean up against a tree trunk, and wait. Feel the energy of the place. Is the wind blowing? What emotions are you feeling? Notice any animals that find their way into the area. Do they stop to look at you? Feel your spiritual essence, your frequency, build up around your heart and then reach it out into the center of the area. Now wait. Do you feel any animal energy connecting with yours? When you do, feel the connection, the emotions of the animal, look at the pictures it sends to you, and, most of all, thank the animal for sharing its energy with you on the level of the Divine. Gently pull your frequency back inside you, knowing that you now share part of this animal's frequency within your spiritual being, just as the animal you connected with now carries part of you with its frequency.

෧෨

Chapter Five

MYTHICAL ANIMALS

Amarok

Element(s): Earth | Primary Color(s): Gray

The amarok, a figure in Inuit mythology, is a giant lone wolf that preyed upon hunters who went out at night. When amarok appears, it means for you to be more self-reliant and independent. While the obstacles you face may be intimidating, you have the courage and strength of character to easily overcome them. Amarok encourages you to connect to your inner huntsman.

The opposite sides of amarok represent the positive and negative situations that are encountered during a lifetime. You can choose to see a glass as half full or half empty, and your choices will be determined by which side of amarok is influencing you. When facing negativity, you can let it affect and influence you or you can be courageous and strong; choosing to walk away from it onto a path of light and positivity. Amarok encourages you to choose wisely and not to let darkness extinguish your light. Amarok warns against harboring negative feelings toward another person just because you may not agree with what they are doing or saying. Once you understand that you can't change people, you can only change yourself, then you will have understood amarok's warning.

Amphisbaena

Element(s): Earth | Primary Color(s): Brown, red

Amphisbaena is a winged serpent with the claws of an eagle and a second head at the end of its tail that eats ants. When Amphisbaena appears, it means you're entering a time of renewal and transformation. If you're in a situation that feels as if you're being emotionally torn or you are experiencing the deep cut of betrayal, Amphisbaena will help you heal quickly and come through the situation even stronger than before. Amphisbaena is believed to have amazing powers of regeneration. If you experience negativity that causes you emotional pain, you too can put yourself back together.

Both of Amphisbaena's heads have a separate brain. This means you can look at situations from two points of view. Amphisbaena's eyes are said to be powerful beams of light that penetrate the darkness. This means your inner light shines into the world. You connect to the light of the universe and the spiritual bond you have with all that is, all that was, and all that will be. While the Amphisbaena can roll, it can also instantly move in opposite directions without having to turn around. This means that you are not limited to only going one way in life.

Basilisk

Element(s): Air, earth | Primary Color(s): Black, green, yellow

Basilisk is the legendary serpent with a white mark on its head that resembles a crown and was considered the king of all serpents. Basilisk symbolizes leadership, self-confidence, and a positive self-esteem. When basilisk appears, it means there is a new leadership opportunity coming your way. You have charisma and people are drawn to your strength and intense personality. You are a natural leader filled with self-confidence and a high self-esteem (but not so much that you come across as a know-it-all). You lead by example and never ask others to do something you wouldn't do yourself. Basilisk means visualizing to gain insight into the best course of action.

Basilisk is extremely venomous, so it is important to remember that your words and actions can cause harm if you strike out in anger. Basilisk warns to have pride in what you do but don't be arrogant about it. Basilisk gives the power, confidence, and faith to move obstacles out of your way. Be careful of how you stare at people because your stare can be intimidating and make others uncomfortable even if you're not meaning it that way.

Bigfoot

Element(s): Earth | Primary Color(s): Black, brown
(depending on region), white

Bigfoot is believed to be a reclusive apelike being that is very difficult to encounter because it hides so well. When Bigfoot appears, it means you're going to face the unknown in some way. Bigfoot means you may encounter some rather large obstacles crossing your path that you weren't expecting. Just as Bigfoot retains total control over who it allows to see it, you also retain control of your life path.

Bigfoot represents fear of the dark and the things that live in the night. When you embrace the light of your being and release the fear that is confining you, then you can move forward into positivity. Bigfoot is an undiscovered creature, which means you've yet to discover all of your intuitive abilities, your life blessings, and your soul purpose. When Bigfoot appears, it is to remind you of the unexplained mysteries in life. Not everything in life can be seen, touched, or completely explained but it still exists. Bigfoot warns to be aware of people who are dangerous to you but hide behind a facade of comfort and interest in your well-being.

Bunyip

Element(s): Earth, water | Primary Color(s): Black, brown

Bunyip is a water spirit monster from Australian Aboriginal mythology. It lives along rivers, watering holes, and in swamps. Bunyip symbolizes supernatural power, disguise, and aggressive behavior. When bunyip appears, it means that someone around you is pretending to be something they're not. This means to be on the lookout for deception in your life. Be particularly aware of the intentions behind words or requests for you to do something.

Bunyip means you work better at night than you do during the day. Some mythology says bunyip hugs its prey to death. This is a sign to examine your relationships. Are you being too clingy or aggressive in your affections because you fear losing the person you're involved with? Or are you not showing enough affection? If you're being too clingy and are holding on too tightly in your relationships, you could kill them because the other person feels smothered. If you're not showing enough affection, then bunyip encourages you to give hugs more often and let the other person know how much you love them.

Cadmean Vixen

Element(s): Earth | Primary Color(s): Black, gray, red

Cadmean vixen (aka Teumessian fox) was an enormous fox destined to never be caught. When Cadmean vixen appears, it means to stop running in circles. While there are times in life when you need to double back to revisit an area where you've already been, if you're continuously going to the past, then you're not making forward progress. Running in circles means you're spending time on aimless, nonproductive activities either because you're having difficulties coming to a solution or because you're procrastinating or putting off tasks that need to be completed.

Cadmean vixen means that when you find yourself going around and around an issue you need to stop, look at the pros and cons, and make a decision without letting others influence how you feel. You may believe they are chasing you into a corner, forcing you to do something you really may not want to do. If that's the case, Cadmean vixen will help you get away so you can think things through and come to your own decision. Cadmean vixen also means to pay more attention to the children in your life.

Caladrius

Element(s): Air | Primary Color(s): White

Caladrius is a snow-white bird that lives in the houses of kings according to Roman mythology. It symbolizes life and death. When caladrius appears, it means to look at your health. If anything has been worrying you, or if you haven't had a physical in a long time, now might be a good time to go to the doctor and get yourself checked out just to make sure all is well. Caladrius means you will be making emotional choices. Are you only spurred into action when you get angry about something and have an I'll show them attitude? If so, is this negatively or positively affecting you? Think about it and if it's a negative result, then decide how you can change the negative into a positive and then make that change.

The death associated with caladrius in the legend is physical, but when it appears to you it doesn't reflect physical death but instead means that something in your life will end and bring about something new. Caladrius warns against taking on more than you can handle. If you think something will harm you or cause you distress, then turn away from the situation just as caladrius turns away from what will harm it.

Cerastes

Element(s): Earth | Primary Color(s): Brown

Cerastes, in Greek mythology, is a serpent that is so flexible it was considered spineless. When Cerastes appears, it means there is falseness around you. Cerastes means to look for jealousy, envy, gossip, and dislike among those you come into contact with on a daily basis. Is someone treating you well and talking bad about you behind your back? This is Cerastes's influence.

Cerastes means to use your intuition and trust in the information you're given to see to the heart of the matter. There are tricksters around you with negative intentions so you need to be on your toes right now. Use stealth to find out what's really going on by being elusive and concealing your investigation. Protect yourself in whatever ways you feel are necessary at this time, especially by building up a wall around your emotions so you're not hurt when someone betrays you. Cerastes means you may be able to stop betrayals before they happen by finding out information and confronting the other person before they can do something emotionally hurtful to you. If you can uncover the intention before the action takes place, you can prevent disaster.

Cetan

Element(s): Air | Primary Color(s): Brown

In Lakota mythology, Cetan is a hawk spirit associated with the east. Cetan symbolizes inner stamina, dedication, swift speed, and intense vision. When Cetan appears, it means you are going to receive messages from the spiritual realm. If you've been working with your spirit guides, angels, or energy animals, you'll notice that the lines of communication will open wide and information starts to flow freely once Cetan appears.

Cetan removes any blockages that may have prevented you from being able to see or hear Spirit clearly. Cetan indicates you will be experiencing changes. Cetan means to be awake, present in your life, and aware. It is a connection to the earth, to your roots, and it is a symbol of the soul. Cetan warns against preying on the weak or taking advantage of others in order to succeed. Cetan reminds you to connect with the warrior spirit, the hero within you, to always move with grace and positivity and act from a place of love. You are a visionary and it's important to retain your vision and goals for the future. Cetan means you will soar to great heights of success in all you attempt.

Chimera

Element(s): Earth, fire | Primary Color(s): Brown, green

In Greek mythology, Chimera is an immortal, unique, three-headed beast, the only one of its kind. It was considered to be of Divine origin. When Chimera appears, it means that you can reach greater heights by combining your knowledge and abilities than by keeping them separated. Chimera means by being persistent you can persevere over any obstacles in your path.

Chimera enables you to live life without limits. This includes the limits others may try to place on you or those you place on yourself. Chimera means you are a creative individual who often thinks outside of the box. Your passion for life and the work you do enables you to excel in whatever areas interest you. Chimera warns that you become bored easily, and if you lose interest it is as if the thing never existed to begin with. It assists when you need to remain strong during chaotic times when your emotions are in turmoil. When you're going through difficult times, Chimera urges you to return to your own Divine source, to the beginnings of your spiritual self, in order to find the strength and fortitude to endure emotional difficulties.

Chupacabra

Element(s): Earth | Primary Color(s): Gray, green

Chupacabra is a cryptid believed to inhabit the Americas. It is known for attacking livestock, primarily goats, and draining them of their blood through three holes in the shape of an inverted triangle. When chupacabra appears, it means that something or someone is draining you. There may be someone in your life who is demanding a lot of your time, whether this is done on purpose or is unintentional. If you're caring for an ill family member, the task will pull on your energy, possibly leaving you exhausted, but it is not an intentional hardship instigated by the sick person.

There may be strains on your finances at this time. You may encounter unexpected bills or expenses and need to tighten your spending patterns for a while. You could also be experiencing a situation where you feel your self-confidence is taking a hit. Chupacabra is symbolic of endings. But with endings come new beginnings. You're entering a new phase of your life, step forward and embrace it. Chupacabra assists when you need to learn to control your temper, be less of a predator, and be less strong willed.

Cockatrice

Element(s): Air, earth | Primary Color(s): Black, brown, green, red, white, multicolored

The mythical flying beast Cockatrice stands on two legs and has the head and feet of a cockerel (rooster) and the body and tail of a dragon. When Cockatrice appears, it means you are independent and adaptable and have a unique perspective. You're a rare individual who often does things unexpected and out of the ordinary to make others happy just because you like seeing their faces light up with joy. You feel particularly drawn to anything that seems magical, inspirational, or enlightening.

Cockatrice's ability to create endings means you are able to see when things are no longer needed in your life. Cockatrice stands on two legs, which is a sign that you stand on your own and take care of yourself. Cockatrice means to enjoy the mornings, even if you're sometimes a night owl. Getting up when the rooster crows can give you new perspectives and fresh ideas as you watch the sun rise. It's a great time to get organized, evaluate your schedule, or get your exercise in before you really get going with your day. It will also boost your mood and enhance your productivity.

Dragon

Element(s): Air, earth, water | Primary Color(s): Black, blue, gold, green, orange, red, white, yellow

Dragon symbolizes strength, good luck, and financial growth. Dragon is a magical being that is physically strong, but it also has strength of character that is shown through its wisdom. When dragon appears, it means this is a prosperous time for you. This prosperity can be connected to material possessions and brings an increase in the things you own or the amount of money you make. Spiritually you'll experience an increase in your intuition, growth along your spiritual path, and connection to your higher purpose.

Dragon means you're open-minded and are drawn to all types of metaphysical and mystical topics. You're at one with your unique spirituality, are accepting of others, and see the beauty in all things. Dragon means you're a leader who has a great deal of presence. You are regal, dignified, and majestic in your approach to life. People are drawn to you because of these qualities. You are intuitively linked to ancient wisdom, which you willingly share with others. Dragon is fearless, is passionate, and has a high sense of adventure.

Visualization with Dragon

Imagine ... You find yourself transported back to medieval times. An enormous dragon is flying above you in slow circles. You can't take your eyes off of the incredible beast. You move out into an open field as the dragon gets lower and lower. It sees you and lands in the field. You feel an affinity for it and walk closer. It regards you with curiosity. You talk to it and reach out to touch its nose. You can hear it speaking in your mind. It has been looking for you to take you back to your own time. You climb on its back and fly home.

☙

Erymanthian Boar

Element(s): Earth | Primary Color(s): Brown

The Erymanthian Boar, in Greek mythology, was a giant boar with very sharp teeth that lived on Mount Erymanthos. When Erymanthian Boar appears, you are about to escape from something that has been holding you back and start over, creating your own new beginning. When Hercules threw the Erymanthian Boar into the sea, the expectation was that it would drown. But the Boar, intent on survival, swam across the sea to Italy. This means, regardless of the conditions you find yourself thrown into, you will find a way to turn a negative into a positive and start again.

Erymanthian Boar gives you the courage to take on tasks you'd rather avoid by encouraging you to put your fear and doubts behind you so you can step up to the job at hand with a sense of determined resolve to see it through to a successful completion. Erymanthian Boar means to look for what's hidden. With new beginnings often come great amounts of growth and changes of perspective. What you once disbelieved you may now hold as truth. What was once unknown is now known. Erymanthian Boar warns against procrastination. Work now to reap your rewards.

Gargoyle

Element(s): Air, earth | Primary Color(s): Black, gray, green, white

In legend, gargoyle is a mythological creature of a winged race that was once human but gave in to its more animalistic and negative basic behaviors. Its wings symbolize its ability to rise above and overcome these behaviors. When gargoyle appears, it means you cannot let the conditions in which you find yourself affect your Divine nature. Sometimes everything in life flows smoothly, is wonderful, and you're filled with joy. Other times the road is rocky, rough, and fills you with sadness.

Gargoyle means to take solace in the silence. Use it to connect to the divinity within you, to embrace your inner self, and pull yourself up out of despair. Gargoyle reflects human potential and the ability to rise above negativity. Legend says the gargoyles on rooftops communicate when the rain or wind passes between their mouths. They can also manipulate water by purifying it, which prevents disease. This cleansing associated with water also applies to you. If you feel drawn to water then spend time around it, drink more of it, and take a relaxing bath in it.

Gremlin

Element(s): Air, earth | Primary Color(s): Black, brown,
green, red, multicolored

Gremlin has its origins in Welsh folklore as creatures named Coranyeidd, spirit creatures who heard everything so no one could keep secrets. When gremlin appears, it means to take responsibility for your own actions. Gremlin is often used as a scapegoat for mistakes instead of the person taking responsibility for doing something wrong. If you've been blaming a gremlin, or anyone else for that matter, for something you did incorrectly or you were supposed to do and didn't complete, now is the time to own up to your actions. If you can fix a past situation, then do it. If not, decide to start owning your actions beginning today.

Gremlin has a mischievous and playful nature, which is a sign you need more fun in your life. You don't have to pull pranks or do negative things like a gremlin is blamed for, but you should implement ways to find more enjoyment and pleasurable things to do on a daily basis. Gremlin means to give credit where credit is due. Legends say gremlins turned on humans when they took credit for what the gremlins did.

Griffin

Element(s): Air, earth | Primary Color(s): Brown, gold, white

Griffin has the body of a lion and the head and wings of an eagle. Its front feet are eagle claws and its back feet are lion paws. Griffin symbolizes power, wisdom, and wealth. When griffin appears, it means you're going to need to be strong in upcoming situations. Griffin represents strength in battle and was often used in coats of arms in ancient and medieval times. Griffin enables you to think quickly on your feet and come up with unique solutions to problems others may not see.

Griffin means you live by your higher purpose and help others reach their own spiritual enlightenment. You are also a guardian of ancient knowledge and can access the Akashic Records. You have intuitive insight and a problem-solving mind, which aids in your ability to see situations from a different perspective. Griffin is a symbol of the Divine and is the guardian of sacred, mysterious libraries and also guards the path to spiritual enlightenment. It will hold you back until you release any negative emotions. It is said that griffin feathers touching the eyelids heal the blind, which means griffin helps your intuitive sight.

Hippogriff

Element(s): Air, earth | Primary Color(s): Brown

Hippogriff is the offspring of a griffin and a horse. The front half looks like an eagle and the back half like a horse. When hippogriff appears, it means you will accomplish what seems impossible. Griffins view horses as prey, and they mate for life. So a griffin mating with a mare, who then foals out a hippogriff, would be an extremely rare event and is associated with love. This is a sign of an impossible situation coming to fruition.

Hippogriff urges you to see extraordinary possibilities in your daily life, to see the Divine in everything around you, and to believe nothing is impossible and you can achieve anything you set out to do. Hippogriff means you are grounded and balanced, and when you love, you love with all of your heart and soul. As a spiritual being filled with light and love, you share these aspects of yourself with those you come into contact with on a daily basis. This allows them to see the same qualities within them-selves. Hippogriff demands respect and urges you to do the same. It assists when you need to bring your dreams to life.

Hydra of Lerna

Element(s): Water | Primary Color(s): Black, brown, green, red

Hydra, also called the Lernaean Hydra in Greek mythology, was a sea serpent with nine heads (the middle one was immortal, venomous, and had poison breath) that guarded the entrance to the underworld. When Hydra appears, it means to look at situations from a different perspective. Hydra had nine heads. That's nine different points of view. When you analyze a situation from multiple perspectives and different possible viewpoints, you can see it in a unique way.

Hydra protected the gateway to the underworld, which means you have a protective nature as well. You can be fierce in the protection of those you care about or causes in which you're involved. Hydra encourages you to be flexible and not too rigid. If you're too rigid and unmoving, you may encounter more difficulties in life than you would if you move with the flow of life. Hydra indicates you are a survivor, able to regenerate yourself and experience abundant energy in your life. People and situations don't usually get your spirits down for long. You're able to bounce back quickly because you see them from different perspectives.

Jackalope

Element(s): Air, earth | Primary Color(s): Brown

In North American folklore, jackalope is a creature born from crossing a jackrabbit and an antelope. It looks like a rabbit with antlers. When jackalope appears, it means to be fearless in competition. Use your intelligence and cunning to come up with ways to win that show you can think outside of the box. Jackalope imitates human voices to aid in its escape. This means you should listen closely to what others say because you might learn something you didn't know.

Jackalope means people see you as shy when in fact you just keep quiet about a lot of things instead of being too talkative. You're really an outgoing person, but you tend to not say things unless you know that what you're saying is correct (because you don't want to be wrong). You're tough and can go the distance in any situation, even if people don't see you that way. Your strong sense of purpose and inner confidence give you an advantage in many different situations. You strive to be the best you can be but aren't above fighting back if necessary. Jackalope means you may be very good at doing impersonations of others.

Jersey Devil

Element(s): Air, earth | Primary Color(s): Brown

According to legend, the Jersey Devil is a cryptid creature that lives in the Pine Barrens of southern New Jersey. When Jersey Devil appears, it means you are fearless in the face of adversity. You have an inner strength you rely on to achieve what you want out of life and to get you through difficult situations. Jersey Devil has quick reflexes, can be invisible to humans, and moves silently through the shadows. You also rely on your quick wit and reflexes to get yourself out of tight spots, you can become invisible to others when it suits your needs, hearing what you need to know without others being aware of your presence, and you easily move within the shadows if necessary. These qualities make you a great detective.

When confronted, you have the knack of evading questions you don't want to answer and are able to hold your own if someone is antagonizing you. It's easy for you to turn a negative situation into a positive one because you're connected to the universal flow. People see you as a quiet but powerful person who gleans great insights from little things that often go unnoticed by others.

Jormungand

Element(s): Water | Primary Color(s): Black, green

Jormungand, according to Old Norse mythology, is a huge snakelike serpent with large fangs and a flat tail that lives in the ocean surrounding Midgard, the realm of human civilization. He grows to be so huge he can wrap himself in a circle around Midgard and grasp his tail in his mouth. When Jormungand appears, it means to get ready for major positive changes in your life. You may be moving to a new location, starting a new job, or beginning a family. Whatever situation you find yourself in, Jormungand means that life as you know it will never be the same after the coming events. This is a time to hold on to your faith, positivity, and cheery attitude. This is a time of rebirth, of growth, and of lifting your expectations. Listen to your higher self, experience the regeneration of your spirituality, connect with your bliss and joy, and live in happiness and love. Jormungand means to live your life with conviction. Stand by what you believe in and those you love. Jormungand warns against stepping back from life and becoming reclusive as you adjust to the changes you'll experience.

Kelpie

Element(s): Water | Primary Color(s): Black, white

Kelpie is a cross between a horse and a fish. The front of the kelpie looks like a horse and has two front hooves, the back is the tail of a fish. When kelpie appears, it means there are storms coming your way, so prepare for rough waters. If a kelpie appears, it means you are connecting with your own spiritual nature, your thoughts and beliefs, to get you through a difficult emotional time. By looking within, you will be able to change any negative emotions you're feeling into positive ones.

Kelpie warns against blaming others for your problems. It's time to break free from anything holding you back, from being emotionally controlled by someone else, and from any restraints you've placed upon yourself. Kelpie is known to misrepresent itself to deceive unsuspecting humans and put them in harm's way. Are you deceiving yourself by thinking that someone will change when you know they will only change when they want to, not because you want them to? Look at all areas of your life to see if you're looking with blinders on instead of seeing situations and people as they truly are.

Kongamato

Element(s): Air | Primary Color(s): Black, red

Kongamato is a creature similar to a pterodactyl that lives in the Jiundu swamps in western Zambia, near the Congo and Angola borders. When Kongamato appears, it means that it is time for you to reach new heights. In order to soar through the sky, you have to be released from the ropes holding you down. This means to look to your past and let go of old habits or fears that are no longer necessary. Kongamato means someone from your past may reappear. Kongamato urges you to seek out the truth so you will gain a better understanding of yourself. That way you can move out of idealizing the past to live in the present.

Kongamato signifies you should let your own inner light shine brightly into the night for all to see. You can be a guiding light to others. Kongamato urges you to deal with any old issues that show up as quickly as you can so they don't pull you down. Fix it and let it go. It also urges you to never give up on your dreams. Fly high, glide at a slow pace, and feel the wind above and beneath you. When you can appreciate the simplicities in every moment then you can truly soar.

Kraken

Element(s): Water | Primary Color(s): Black, gray, green

Kraken, in Scandinavian mythology, is a giant sea creature with a body so big (about one mile long) it looked like an island if it was floating near the surface. When Kraken appears to you, it is a sign of upcoming abundance and an increase in wealth in all areas of your life. Kraken would trap fish by belching and releasing food into the water. This is symbolic of manifestation and bringing what you desire to you. The Kraken desired a meal, so it brought the fish to it. What can you do to bring the things you want to you? Begin by practicing creative visualization and manifestation to create abundance in your life.

Kraken means to be brave and courageous in all that you do. Face situations head-on instead of backing away from them. You are self-reliant, just like Kraken, and usually don't depend on anyone but yourself. Kraken urges you to access the ancient knowledge within you because it will lead to a spiritual awakening. Kraken means to make sure you're getting enough sleep and resting whenever you can. You tend to do a lot in your life and can get run down if you're not resting enough.

TIP 6

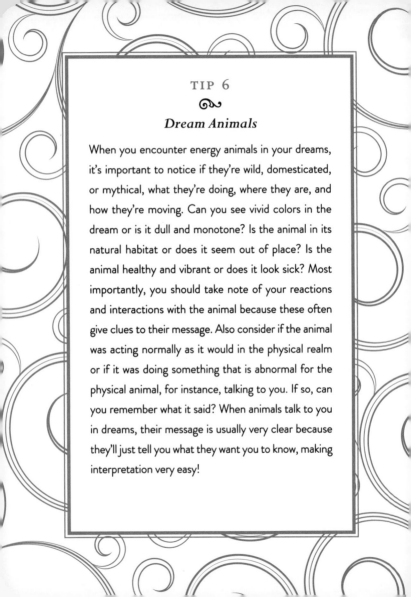

Dream Animals

When you encounter energy animals in your dreams, it's important to notice if they're wild, domesticated, or mythical, what they're doing, where they are, and how they're moving. Can you see vivid colors in the dream or is it dull and monotone? Is the animal in its natural habitat or does it seem out of place? Is the animal healthy and vibrant or does it look sick? Most importantly, you should take note of your reactions and interactions with the animal because these often give clues to their message. Also consider if the animal was acting normally as it would in the physical realm or if it was doing something that is abnormal for the physical animal, for instance, talking to you. If so, can you remember what it said? When animals talk to you in dreams, their message is usually very clear because they'll just tell you what they want you to know, making interpretation very easy!

Ladon (Python)

Element(s): Earth | Primary Color(s): Black, brown, green

Ladon, in Greek mythology, was a hundred-headed serpent dragon that guarded the golden apples of the Hesperides. When Ladon appears, it means to be on guard because someone may try to take something that is yours. This could be as simple as someone taking an ink pen off of your desk or taking your lunch from the refrigerator, or it could be very complicated. Ladon means to watch your back and be extra diligent about safety for the next few weeks. Ladon will protect you, but you should also heighten your awareness.

Ladon means you will have new opportunities coming your way that will increase your financial status. The golden apples Ladon protected were sacred and valuable. This means your own financial value will increase. Make sure you're looking for these opportunities so you don't miss them. Ladon means you're a formidable opponent at work. You enjoy the competitiveness of a business environment and fearlessly work to be successful. Ladon was passionate about its job of protecting the golden apples and fought to the end to keep them safe. You're just as passionate in every aspect of your life.

Loch Ness Monster

Element(s): Earth, water | Primary Color(s): Gray

The Loch Ness Monster, commonly referred to as Nessie, is a cryptid lake monster that lives in Loch Ness in the Scottish Highlands. The Loch Ness Monster symbolizes ancient knowledge, intuitive insight, and universal connections. When the Loch Ness Monster appears, it means to pay attention to the natural world around you. You are intuitively connected to the elements at this time, especially anything to do with water.

Since the Loch Ness Monster is rarely seen, this is a sign to connect to the part of your inner self that you often avoid. In order to reach spiritual enlightenment, you must consider every part of yourself—your faults as well as your gifts. Analyzing your faults will enable you to find ways to turn them into gifts, furthering your spiritual growth. The Loch Ness Monster encourages you to use your intuitive insightfulness to connect to deeper, more ancient knowledge. It can be elusive, so you must look to your inner essence and higher self with awareness and conviction, and be pure in heart. Nessie assists when you need inspiration, hope, and strength. Loch Ness Monster represents the uplifting of spirit.

Nandi Bear

Element(s): Earth | Primary Color(s): Brown, red

Nandi Bear in legend is a cryptid that lived in East Africa. When Nandi Bear appears, it means to use your brain and your intelligence to come to reasonable decisions. The Nandi Bear was known to only eat the brains of its victims. This also indicates you are connected to ancient knowledge. By accessing this knowledge, you can understand more about human nature, life, and the spiritual. It is your divine right to grow in spirit.

Nandi Bear has the ability to hide where no one will find it, but it also has a warrior spirit. It is filled with power, is resourceful, and is confident that it will succeed. While it does have the brain-eating zombie thing going on and is an unpredictable, violent beast, it also lives in harmony within its own world and finds balance within itself. You too are resourceful, filled with confidence in your abilities, and have the spirit of a hero. You will fight for those who need your help. Just leave the brain eating to the Nandi Bear. It assists when you need to connect with your inner courage to be victorious. Nandi Bear can help you connect with the strength of the warrior within you.

Nemean Lion

Element(s): Earth | Primary Color(s): Gold

In Greek mythology, the Nemean Lion was a shapeshifter that took women from the towns as hostages. When Nemean Lion appears, it is a warning that a threat is nearby. Nemean Lion means to be alert, pay attention, and be ready to fight for what you want or believe in if necessary. This threat could come in the form of a person who disguises his or her intentions, just as the Nemean Lion pretended to be something it wasn't in order to obtain its predatory goals.

The Nemean Lion represents your own inner strength and bravery. You're not afraid to be assertive in order to obtain what you want. You are courageous and will step forward in situations where others cower. There is valor and fortitude within you. People look up to you for your strength and wisdom. Nemean Lion warns against being too aggressive or presenting yourself as something you're not. Be true to yourself to achieve all that you want. When you purposefully deceive others to gain your own ends, that's when you'll experience defeat. It takes bravery to be honest and forthright. Nemean Lion assists when you need to deal with an overpowering authority figure in your life.

Ogopogo

Element(s): Water | Primary Color(s): Green

Ogopogo is a sea serpent that lived in Okanagan Lake in British Columbia, Canada. When Ogopogo appears, it's a sign of transformation and to look for deeper meanings in your life. In First Nations mythology, a native possessed by demons killed Kan-He-Kan, a local wise man. The gods captured the murderer and transformed him into a serpent as punishment. They threw the serpent into the lake, condemning him to remain there forever. Since that time, there have been many sightings of the beast that quite often appears like a log but moves against the water currents.

In 1989, Ogopogo was given protected wildlife status, which makes it illegal to harm it. This means to protect yourself from negativity as you discover new ideals and how to use latent abilities on your spiritual path. There is always negativity in the world, it is how you handle it that either blocks your path or allows you to move along without interruption. Ogopogo's transformation from man to beast indicates you too will change as you walk your path. How you transform will depend on your outlook, intention, and connection to the truth within your soul.

Owlman

Element(s): Air, earth | Primary Color(s): Brown, gray

Owlman is an oversized owl with red, glowing, slanted eyes, pointy ears, a beak-shaped mouth, large wings, sharp talons, and a seven-foot-tall body. When Owlman appears, it is a sign to rise above negativity. People saw Owlman suddenly appear standing right in front of them, up in the trees, or flying around the top of church towers. Once seen, Owlman would often rise up in the air and fly out of sight. This signifies being able to lift yourself up with your own inner strength to rise above obstacles appearing along your path.

Owlman would pursue people, quietly and unseen, before it appeared. This is a sign for you to pursue your dreams. You don't have to tell everyone what you're doing, but, like Owlman, you can be silent in your pursuit until you've realized your dreams. Owlman sees in the dark. You too can see what is hidden when you're paying attention. Owlman is often considered an illusion, a being that was made up out of fear of the unknown. This means to look for illusions in your life. Owlman assists when you need to find your way. Owlman, while known to frighten, can also lead you in a different direction.

Pegasus

Element(s): Air, earth | Primary Color(s): White

Pegasus is a divine stallion with wings that brought lightning and thunderbolts from Olympus to Zeus. Pegasus symbolizes being in service to others, spirituality, and travel. When Pegasus appears, it means you desire to rise above your ordinary way of life in the physical realm to seek knowledge in the spiritual realm and attain soul growth. It was believed that each time Pegasus struck his hoof on the ground an inspirational spring was born. Pegasus means you have the innate ability to transform negativity into positivity through your connection to the spiritual.

Pegasus is a beautiful, pure being filled with gentleness and grace. This means you have the same qualities within you, which draws people to you. They sense you are down-to-earth, transparent, and willing to listen and help them with their problems. Your emotional stability helps you give them unbiased guidance that inspires and elevates their own spiritual nature. Pegasus warns against purposefully manipulating situations or other people to get your own way, blaming others for your actions, or playing on another's emotions. He assists when you need inspiration.

Phoenix

Element(s): Air, fire | Primary Color(s): Orange, purple, red, yellow

The Phoenix symbolizes birth, living life, death, and rebirth. It is the ability to overcome hard times and loss to bounce back better than before. People often say they will rise from the ashes like the Phoenix, meaning they'll get through whatever tough experience they're involved with and will rise out of it better than before. It's survival at its finest through internal transformation and regeneration.

A heightened sense of spiritual awareness, intuition, sense of being, and feeling connected to the universe and all within it are traits of the Phoenix. It often appears during times of transition. Doors may shut but keep watch for the opening windows. You are about to experience a time of rebirth, letting go of the old and embracing the new. It means to rise above difficulties, remain true to your inner essence, and look at situations using your intuition. Keep the faith that everything will work out the way it is supposed to and light will result from any darkness you are experiencing. Stay strong with your convictions and remain true to your inner self and your beliefs.

Sea-Goat

Element(s): Water | Primary Color(s): Brown, green

Sea-goat mythology says that the god Chronos created Pricus, the first sea-goat from which all others came. The sea-goat is half goat and half fish, is very intelligent, can speak, and was favored by the gods. When sea-goat appears, it means to let go of something or someone you've been trying to control. This means you may think you have the best interest of someone at heart when you try to control their actions, but you can't control someone else. Once they reach adulthood, each person has to be free to make his or her own decisions and follow his or her own path of spiritual growth and enlightenment. There will be mistakes made along the way, but that's when the most spiritual growth happens. When you try to control someone else, it is usually due to your own fears and insecurities. Once you recognize these traits in yourself, as Pricus did, then you can stop being controlling and allow things to move forward as the universe intended. Sea-goat assists when you need to have patience, be disciplined, and be loyal.

Shisa

Element(s): Earth | Primary Color(s): Black, blue, brown, gold, gray, green, indigo, orange, pink, purple, red, silver, turquoise, white, yellow, multitude of color combinations

Shisa are wards symbolizing protection and keeping evil spirits away. When shisa appears, it means now is the time to deepen your connection to universal knowledge and your higher self.

The shisa represents Buddhist symbolism in that the shisa with the open mouth is meant to be shaping the "a" sound while the shisa with the closed mouth is meant to be shaping the "un" sound. When said together they create *a-un*, which, when translated from Hindu to Indian, is the word *om*. In Buddhism, om represents the sound of universal vibration. Om is often used in meditation and in yoga because it is a highly spiritual sound that helps connect your creative inner power to the frequency of the universe and, in turn, universal knowledge. When you're facing an obstacle that is much larger than you are, reach inside, gather your voice and courage, and face the obstacle head-on to overcome it. Shisa warns against acting in anger but the emotion of anger can spur you to accomplish your goal.

Sleipnir

Element(s): Air, earth, water | Primary Color(s): Gray

Sleipnir is an enormous enchanted horse with eight legs in Norse mythology. When Sleipnir appears, it means you will be very busy doing a lot of things at once, so you feel as if you're moving at a great rate of speed. It may also mean you will be traveling.

Sleipnir can mean that you are on a quest of spiritual enlightenment and will receive assistance from many helping spirits on your journey. Sleipnir warns against being ruthless in your search for more knowledge or wisdom. Don't be cold or unfeeling in your pursuits but instead seek the truth by connecting to your emotions. The spiritual journey is one filled with wonder, awe, and inspiration. If you're feeling negative emotions or darkness on your search, then you're on the wrong path. Look for the light and follow Sleipnir out of darkness. Sleipnir assists when you need to find inspiration to be more creative. If you feel blocked, just thinking about Sleipnir can boost your creativity. How can Sleipnir's qualities inspire you? If you're seeking adventure, Sleipnir can help you find places and exciting activities that will engage and fulfill you.

Stymphalian Bird (Roc)

Element(s): Air | Primary Color(s): Gold

Stymphalian bird has sharp, metallic feathers, poisonous feces, and a bronze beak. In Greek mythology, it was considered a man-eater that threw its feathers at victims. When Stymphalian bird appears, it means to think of unique ways to achieve your goals. When you apply creative thinking to your life, you can achieve things that others think are impossible while keeping negativity at bay.

Stymphalian bird assists when you need to purposefully put an end to something so new opportunities and people can enter your life. Stymphalian bird made a mess of everything it touched. If you've been feeling as if your life is upside down and you're making a mess of everything you touch, then you may be receiving a message from Stymphalian bird to take a closer look around you. In order for renewal to occur, there first has to be some kind of ending, whether it's in the form of destroying any negativity that's holding you back, ending a relationship, or letting go of something that's no longer serving you. Stymphalian bird is with you to help with the ending so you can move forward into renewal, meeting new people, and experiencing new opportunities.

Thunderbird

*Element(s): Air | Primary Color(s): Black, blue, green, orange,
red, yellow, all arranged so it's multicolored*

In Native American mythology, thunderbird is a supernatural being that carries around glowing snakes and creates thunderstorms at will when it flies. When thunderbird appears, it means you will be going through a time of transition, shifting from your present form to another in regard to your spirituality and beliefs. Thunderbird is revered because it would guard a sacred fire or carry dew on its back that, when released, would restore fertility to the earth.

Thunderbird has a dual nature. While it is protective and will fight other supernatural beings on behalf of man, it can also be destructive due to the storms it creates. When thunderbird appears, it means you are protected from negative energy, but you also need to be careful of instigating change that comes from a place of negativity. When this happens, you will experience delays and possibly regrets for your actions. Cling to the positive during your transformations. Thunderbird assists when you need to conceal yourself, a project you're working on, or a secret you're keeping.

Unicorn

Element(s): Earth, water | Primary Color(s):White

The unicorn symbolizes purity, innocence, faith, intuition, and enchantment. It is all that is right within the universe, and it is a connection to the higher realms of spirituality. It signifies the higher self, a pure heart, and a loving, gentle, and giving nature. Peace and inner calm, righteousness, and belief in things others may not see are also characteristics of unicorn.

Unicorn often appears when it's time to connect to your core essence, inner being, and higher self. It can mean your spirit guides are trying to reach you but you're not listening. When you see unicorn, stop what you're doing and listen telepathically for unique messages. It means to believe in yourself and have faith that everything will work out how the universe intends. Connecting with unicorn means to delve into your own exceptional creativity and to open yourself to the enchanting ways of the mystical realms, to believe in your intuition and psychic abilities. It means it's time to experience spiritual growth and to discover the mysteries of the universe. You are pure of heart and connected to the Divine. Unicorn helps you see with a sense of wonder and awe.

VISUALIZATION WITH UNICORN

Imagine ... You find yourself walking through a beautiful forest filled with greenery, moss, and the shade from the trees. You come upon a waterfall and there at the edge of the pool of water at its base stands a unicorn. Its energy flows across the water toward you and dances around you as if filled with stardust. It is light yet extremely powerful, so much so that it takes your breath away. You stare at this majestic creature in wonder and awe. You feel such a strong connection to the unicorn that you step into the pool of water and begin to swim toward it. As you do, the unicorn enters the water, where you meet. The unicorn nuzzles your face and then tips its head to guide you toward its back. You climb on and hold on to its neck as it swims back to its side of the pool. The unicorn slowly walks into the forest and finds a large bed of moss, where it lies down. You slip off its back and rest your head against its withers. You're filled with song and start to sing to the unicorn. It turns to look at you and touches its horn to your chest above your heart. You're instantly filled with love and a sense that all is right within the universe.

᙭

White Stag

Element(s): Earth | Primary Color(s):White

White stag symbolizes spiritual growth, prophecy, and the beginning of a quest. In Celtic myth, the white stag appears when the otherworld is close by or when someone is doing something that is improper and unacceptable. It is symbolic of the universal life forces of creation. When white stag appears, it means you're about to experience extreme spiritual growth. What was unknown will become known. You will experience a leap in your intuition, an expansion of your abilities, and access to ancient knowledge. This allows you a deeper connection to your inner essence and higher self.

White stag appears during times of transitions to lend you its power, protection, and sense of perception. It will also keep you grounded as you acclimate to your newfound connection to higher thoughts and ideals. White stag means to keep your sense of purity, sensitivity, and kindness. For if you maintain these qualities, you will be rewarded with great abundance, renewal, and an increased sensitivity that all is connected. White stag means you will have the endurance and strength needed as you adjust to your acknowledgment of universal life forces.

Visualization at a Moment's Notice

Sometimes you need to connect to an animal because it suddenly appears in the flesh, surprising you. When this happens, you don't have time to find a reference book and look up the meaning of the animal. Instead, you need to act fast in the moment and do your research later. The initial energy connection with the animal is most important at this time. When an animal appears out of the blue, immediately stop what you're doing and focus on the animal. Often it will already be looking at you. Watch it for a moment, let your intuition guide you as you connect with it through pictures and telepathic words. Feel your internal vibration begin to elevate until it reaches a high frequency surrounding your heart. Now extend your energy toward the animal and wait for its response. Once the animal connects with your energy, make sure you take note of any words or phrases that you hear that can be helpful in a situation you're dealing with or any type of guidance that is offered. As the energy passes between you, the message will be delivered to you so be alert and attuned to it.

CONCLUSION

As I've discussed throughout this book, animal frequency is a Divine connection to the animal kingdom. It's important to trust in your abilities when combining your frequency to that of your energy animals. Empathy, telepathy, and intuition are especially important so you can feel the deepest connection possible. Your energy animals *want* to share their frequency with you; they want to guide and assist you on your spiritual path. You must believe in yourself and trust that what you hear, see, and feel are messages from your energy animal. Don't doubt or second-guess yourself. Instead, trust in your first impression; it will always be correct. There is no limit to the success you will attain when connecting your energy to the animal kingdom. I hope you enjoy your journey into the world of spirit animals and animal frequency.

Bibliography

Alderton, David. *The Encyclopedia of Animals*. New York: Chartwell Books, 2013.

Alexander, Skye. *The Secret Power of Spirit Animals*. Avon, MA: Adams Media, 2013.

Allen, Judy. *Fantasy Encyclopedia*. Boston: Kingfisher, 2005.

Andrews, Ted. *Animal-Speak: The Spiritual & Magical Powers of Creatures Great & Small*. Woodbury, MN: Llewellyn Publications, 2004.

Angell, Madeline. *America's Best Loved Wild Animals*. New York: Bobbs-Merrill Company, 1975.

Bulfinch, Thomas. *Bulfinch's Mythology: The Age of Fable / The Age of Chivalry / Legends of Charlemagne*. New York: Didactic Press, 2015.

Burnie, David, and Don E. Wilson. *Animal: The Definitive Visual Guide to the World's Wildlife*. New York: Dorling Kindersley, 2001.

Cheung, Theresa. *The Element Encyclopedia of 20,000 Dreams*. New York: Barnes and Noble, by arrangement with HarperElement, 2006.

Chevalier, Jean, and Alain Gheerbrant. *A Dictionary of Symbols*. London: Penguin Books, 1996.

Dempsey, Colin. *The Ultimate Encyclopedia of Mythical Creatures*. United Kingdom: Kandour Ltd, USA: Barnes & Noble Books, 2006.

Edmonds, Margot, and Ella E. Clark. *Voices of the Winds: Native American Legends*. New York: Facts on File, 1989.

Farmer, Steven D. *Animal Spirit Guides*. Carlsbad, CA: Hay House, 2006.

Goldworthy, Brigit. *Totem Animal Messages: Channelled Messages from the Animal Kingdom*. Bloomington, IN: Balboa Press, 2013.

Jackson, Tom. *Animals of the World*. London: Anness Publishing, 2014.

Meyer, Regula. *Animal Messengers: An A-Z Guide to Signs and Omens in the Natural World*. Rochester, VT: Bear & Company, 2015.

Seidelmann, Sarah Bamford. *What the Walrus Knows*. Sarah Seidelmann LLC, 2013.

Stevens, Jose, and Lena Stevens. *Secrets of Shamanism*. New York: Avalon Books, 1988.

Zolar. *Zolar's Encyclopedia of Omens, Signs and Superstitions*. New York: Prentice Hall Press, 1989.